D1035510

A FLOWER
DOES NOT TALK
Zen Essays

by

ABBOT ZENKEI SHIBAYAMA
Nanzenji Monastery
Kyoto, Japan

Translated by
SUMIKO KUDO

CHARLES E. TUTTLE COMPANY
Rutland, Vermont   Tokyo, Japan

Representatives

Continental Europe: BOXERBOOKS, INC., *Zurich*

British Isles: PRENTICE-HALL INTERNATIONAL, INC., *London*

Australasia: BOOK WISE (AUSTRALIA) PTY. LTD.
104-108 Sussex Street, Sydney 2000

Published by the Charles E. Tuttle Company, Inc.
of Rutland, Vermont & Tokyo, Japan
with editorial offices at
2-6, Suido 1-chome, Bunkyo-ku, Tokyo, Japan
Copyright in Japan, 1970, by
The Charles E. Tuttle Company, Inc.
All rights reserved
First edition, 1970
Eleventh printing, 1985
Library of Congress Catalog Card No. 79-109404
International Standard Book No. 0-8048-0884-8

PRINTED IN JAPAN

CONTENTS

147503

PREFACE

The whole world today, both East and West, seems to be going through a period of convulsion, a time of travail, as it seeks to give birth to a new culture. There cannot be one simple cause for the tensions in so many parts of the world, but one of the major factors may be that while remarkable progress has been made in the use of new scientific knowledge, we human beings have not developed sufficiently spiritually and ethically to meet the new conditions.

It is most urgently required, therefore, that we must work to create a new human culture by striving for a truer understanding of humanity and a higher level of spirituality. We must attain a higher level of personality so that we can cope with the brilliant scientific achievements of modern times.

Zen presents a unique spiritual culture in the East, highly refined in its long history and traditions, and I believe it has universal and fundamental values that can contribute toward creating a new spiritual culture in our time. The important point about Zen is, however, that we should understand it, experience it, and live it in the varying circumstances of our everyday life. Small and insignificant as my existence and work as a Zen Roshi may be, I believe that they contribute to the infinite future.

Five years ago, at the kind invitation of The Hazen Foundation, I made my first lecture trip to the United States. Since then on four different occasions I have had the privilege of talking with students and professors at several American colleges and universities. On each trip, as we came to know each other better, I have come to realize more clearly the differences and unique characteristics of Eastern and Western traditions. We should not too easily conclude that there is just one Truth, and that East and West are after all the same. If, however, we are awakened to our true humanity, we will realize that at the bottom of all the differences there is the fountainhead which is the basis for the happiness of all mankind. I am grateful for the invaluable opportunities to get in close touch with the people in the West, not only for the sake of superficial cultural exchange, but because from these experiences has come the significant realization that we are all living as the same kind of human beings in this present moment in history and working for a new human culture together.

I should also like to express our appreciation for the assistance given by The Hazen Foundation in publishing this volume. This book includes several essays written on different occasions: some are lectures given at various universities in the United States, some are texts used for seminars, and some are in the form of light prose, for I believe that Zen can be savoured and enjoyed in such a form, too. Although there are some repetitions, I have decided to present these essays as they were originally composed.

It was Dr. Daisetz T. Suzuki who persuaded me to make my first trip abroad five years ago. I feel especially honoured to include in this English volume an introduction by Dr. Suzuki. It moves me deeply to think that this introduction was the final work penned by Dr. Suzuki at the end of his extraordinary life of ninety-five years. I learned later that upon completion of this introduction he was taken ill the following day, and passed away early the next morning on July 12th, 1966. Even now this expression of Dr. Suzuki's deep friendship and the wondrous workings of the Dharma relationship fill my heart with gratitude.

Thus, the friendship and gracious intentions of our various good friends are contained in this book. I sincerely hope that it will, even in

7

a small way, help to promote real understanding between East and West.

Zenkei Shibayama
Nanzenji Monastery, Kyoto

INTRODUCTION

Zen claims to be "a specific transmission outside the scripture and to be altogether independent of verbalism," but it is Zen Masters who
are most talkative and most addicted to writings
of all sorts. Almost every Master of note has
left what is known as "Sayings" (J. *goroku* or
C. *yü-lu*) which is more or less filled with para-
doxical expressions altogether off the ordinary
logical line of human understanding. The Masters seem to be particularly delighted to lead the
readers to bewilderment with their apparently
irrational and often irrelevant utterances. But
the fact is these utterances issue from the Masters' most kind and loving heartedness as they
wish to open for their students the higher way
of observing things enabling the latter to rid
themselves of the entangling network of relati-
vity. It is indeed because of these entanglements
that we are sinking deeper and deeper into the
abyss of intellectual confusions and affective
embarrassments.

Rev. Zenkei Shibayama, author of this book,
is the Abbot of the Nanzenji Monastery in
Kyoto. As a good Zen Master he talks and
writes, though he knows that the flower does

9

not talk, nor does it write; and the book here rendered into English by Miss Sumiko Kudo, one of his promising disciples, is a prologue attached to a collection of the Abbot's talks occasionally given to his students and to the general audience. He tells us here what Zen is and how it expresses itself by quoting the old masters liberally from *The Transmission of the Lamp.* This book serves as a good introduction to the study of Zen for English speaking peoples of the West.

One of the stories quoted here from Nansen (Nan-ch'üan P'u-yüan, 南 泉 普 願 748–834) characteristically demonstrates a master's attitude towards life and gives us, even of today, a fine example, teaching us how to live Zen. I like this story very much, and wish our readers to especially keep it in mind when pursuing the study of Zen.

When Nansen was working in the field cutting grass with his monks, a travelling monk asked him, "Where is the road to the Nansen Monastery?" The traveller of course did not know that the man he so asked was the Master himself of the Nansen. The latter then nonchalantly held out the sickle he was using and said, "I paid 30 pieces of money for this!" as if he did not hear the question the traveller wished to have answered. It goes without saying that the Master of the Nansen knew perfectly well what the traveller was expecting, but he wished even more to make him realize that Zen's business is not to accumulate abstract knowledge, or to be versed in devious ways of philosophical discussion. Zen is to live a concrete life of this very moment. Hence not the road to the philosophical understanding at the Nansen Monastery, but the actual sickle in hand.

We may presume that the travelling monk was by no means a novice in Zen, but one with a certain experience. He thus wanted to see what Nansen would say and went on: "I am not asking about the cost of your instrument. What I want is the road leading to the Nansen." The Master again apparently ignoring the question, at least in its literal sense, said, "It cuts very well."

One of the most remarkable features of Zen is that it is far from being mystical, quizzical or argumentative but altogether practical, matter-of-fact and firmly stands on solid ground. Another remarkable characteristic of Zen is that Zen people do not build up an artificial gradation among them, and that when they work they all partake in the work regardless of age, elder or novice. Master Hyakujo (Pai-chang Huai-hai, 百丈懷海, 720-814) says: "A day of no work is a day of no eating," and he was a strict observer of the motto.

There are some Western critics of Zen who contend that the Oriental approach to Zen does not necessarily apply to the Western way of thinking and that therefore the West must have or discover its own method whereby Zen can be readily made understandable for them. This is true in one way, but not at all in another way. To be sure the East, that is China and Japan, has had a long history of Zen, and "Zen" is a familiar word to them, and "satori" is not a strange and inaccessible experience. It is imagined that the East is, therefore, naturally at an advantage in this respect. For the Western people, however, this is not the case, and it is thought that their approach must be different.

Superficially, this may sound reasonable. But the fact is, Zen is as remote for the Easterner as it is for the Westerner when Zen tells us to change or reverse our usual way of understanding. This is to say, Zen teaches that in order to understand a mountain to be a mountain in the Zen way, this experience is to be negated first—a mountain is not a mountain— and it is only when this negation is understood that the affirmation "a mountain is a mountain" becomes Reality. This identity of contradiction is at the basis of all Zen thought however bizarre and irrational they may appear to a Westerner as well as an Easterner.

In any case let us not forget that Zen always aspires to make us directly see into Reality itself, that is, be Reality itself, so that we can say along with Meister Eckhart that "Christ is born every minute in my soul," or that "God's Isness is my Isness." Let us keep this in our minds as we endeavour to understand Zen as explained here by Rev. Zenkei Shibayama.

Daisetz T. Suzuki

Matsugaoka Bunko, Kamakura

CHARACTERISTICS OF ZEN

As you know, Buddhism originated in India about 2,500 years ago, founded by the Indian saint Sakyamuni Buddha. In the course of its long history it was taken to various areas of Asia and developed in different ways in each country, being much influenced by the indigenous culture of each land.

Briefly explained, Buddhism consists of two basic elements. One is "the incomparable, perfect, and supreme *satori*," which Sakyamuni Buddha attained after long years of hard searching. This true *satori* is the core of all Buddhist teachings. It is the life and spirit of Buddhism. The second element consists of the various teachings of Sakyamuni Buddha during the forty-nine years of his life after his attainment of *satori*, the teachings by which he demonstrated and explained the *satori* he had experienced.

Thus, Buddhism is based on Sakyamuni Buddha's religious experience, *satori*, and his teachings are expressions and explanations of this *satori* experience. Of course, these two were fused into one in Sakyamuni Buddha's per-

14

sonality, and neither should be taken up independently of the other. In the course of time, however, some people came to think that they might reach *satori* by merely studying and accepting various teachings of Sakyamuni Buddha, and this resulted in the founding of many schools and sects in Buddhism. On the other hand, there were people who thought that the rise of different sects and schools showed an alienation from the true spirit of Buddhism, which is *satori*, and they emphasized the necessity of transmitting the *satori* experience of the founder, which is, after all, the basis of all his teachings.

Zen can be explained as a school which insists on the direct transmission of the *satori* experience itself as the very core of all Buddhist teachings. While most Buddhist schools rely on some particular teachings or sutras left by Sakyamuni, Zen is based on *satori*, the religious experience of Sakyamuni, and regards all of his teachings and explanations as of secondary importance.

Master Eisai (1141-1215) who introduced Zen into Japan, described the position and the significance of Zen in relation to other Buddhist schools when he said, "It is the foundation of Buddhism and is the basis of all sects and schools." He thus defined Zen as the very spirit and source of the Buddhism in which all the schools are embraced.

Satori is the religious basis of Sakyamuni Buddha's personality as the Buddha, and his teachings are its expressions, explanations, or descriptions. It is natural that Zen, which is founded on the *satori* experience, calls itself "the Foundation of Buddhism," and insists on its all-inclusive character as the basis for other Buddhist schools.

Thus, Zen can be accepted in the broad sense as Zen itself, or the Truth itself, apart from its narrow sectarian interpretation as a school of Buddhism. When Zen is seen in such a broad sense, Zen means the Truth, or the Absolute; it is not limited to Buddhism alone, but is the basis of all religions and all philosophies. In this sense, Zen does not remain simply the core of Buddhism, but it works to deepen and revive any religion or philosophy. For instance, there can be Christian Zen, or Taoistic Zen; there can be Zen interpretations of Christianity or of Taoism.

Once a British gentleman came to see my own teacher and decided to study under him. The *koan* my teacher gave to this British gentleman was a famous Christian passage, "Blessed are the poor in spirit." Or, St. Paul's "The outer man perishes, but the inner man is revived day by day" can be a Zen *koan*.

A Zen text tells us that when a Confucian named Kosangoku came to study under the Zen Master Maido, the Master gave him as his *koan* the famous Confucian saying, "Do you think that I am hiding *It* from you? There is nothing that I keep away from you." Another famous Confucian saying, "Tao—just Oneness all through," is today accepted as a Zen *koan*.

Dr. Daisetz T. Suzuki, in his essay entitled "Kabir's Zen," introduced a poem by Kabir, the fifteenth-century Indian mystic. I still remember a few lines from the poem which are to the following effect: "Just one word. There can be no second word. Yet with this One Word you removed all the restrictions from me." I was interested in these lines because they almost exactly echo a Zen *mondo*: "A monk asked Master Seppo, 'What is the First Word?' The Master was silent. The monk went on to another Master, Chosho, and told him the story. Chosho said to the monk, 'You are already the man of the second word.' "

Because of its transcendental and fundamental nature, Zen can be understood and accepted in any field of human activity, going beyond the sectarian differences of religions and philosophies. In Japan, Zen is appreciated without any particular religious connotations.

17

From olden days, intellectuals in Japan have been interested in Zen as a high and refined cultural value, not necessarily as a traditional religious faith. In the course of the seven hundred years after Zen was introduced to Japan, it helped to develop a unique culture of Japan which is today called Zen culture. In this sense, Zen is accepted by the Japanese people as a kind of creative cultural spirit rather than as a school of religion.

Due to its transcendental and fundamental nature, Zen is not restricted by any fixed ideas or customs, but expresses itself freely, making creative use of words and ideas. This may point out a significant direction for the development of culture in the East and the West in the future. What I mean by this is that there seem to be two different senses in which we talk about mutual understanding, or unity of Eastern and Western culture. One is on the simple level of exchange where East and West adopt whatever is good in the other's culture to make up for whatever is lacking and thus to improve their own culture. Another sense is that of deeper and more fundamental appreciation, where both East and West become aware of their unique traditions and culture and then seek the fundamental basis of their differences. In this way their own culture may be deepened and given new significance and life, based on Truth fundamental for all mankind. Zen can best contribute toward exchange in this latter sense.

Up to this point in this essay I have sought to explain the position of Zen in Buddhism and to indicate the role it can play in religion, philosophy, and culture. In Japan today there are many people who insist that a distinction should be made between the Zen school of Buddhism and genuine Zen itself. They maintain that Zen as the Truth itself, in the broadest sense, should be understood and used by all mankind because it can help build and refine the character of the individual and can deepen thought.

THE FOUR MAXIMS

There are four maxims which have traditionally been accepted as explaining the characteristics and ideals of Zen. I now turn to a discussion of these four sayings in an attempt to clarify the characteristics of Zen. They were originally in simple Chinese phrases:

1. *Transmission outside scriptures*
2. *Not relying on letters*
3. *Pointing directly to one's Mind*

4. *Attainment of Buddhahood by seeing into one's Nature**

It is not known who first used these four maxims of Zen but it must have been in the early Tang dynasty, that is, in the seventh century in China, when Zen came gradually to be appreciated by the Chinese people. Zen monks who followed Bodhidharma's teachings in those days rejected the scholastic Buddhist reliance upon sutra studies and maintained that *satori* experience should be the very life and spirit of Buddhism. It may have been those monks who first started using these four lines as their religious maxims.

Transmission outside scriptures

In Buddhism there are many scriptures that were left by Sakyamuni Buddha at various times and various places during his life. In the course of history, many schools of Buddhism were established, based on particular scriptures. In time, scholars made scholastic studies of these scriptures and it was observed that they tended to place too much importance on the metaphysical or philosophical interpretations of the sutras.

---

* 教外別伝，不立文字，直指人心，見性成仏

The scriptures, however, were originally writings trying to explain the *satori* experience which Sakyamuni Buddha personally attained. It is therefore the *satori* experience that can give life to these scriptures. It is impossible to attain *satori* by reading the sutras on the scholastic level. Once an experience is expressed in a conceptual form, it assumes its own objectivity which can be independently treated. Thus there is the danger of misunderstanding the concept as the experiential fact itself, and the experience itself will be forgotten and finally be dead. Zen is flatly against such a tendency and strongly warns us that we should not be attached to any of the scriptures which are likely to be lifeless records.

In *Dento-roku* (The Transmission of the Lamp) we have the following *mondo*: A scholar monk who was known as a good commentator on the sutras once came to see Zen Master Enkan. Enkan asked the visitor, "What sutra do you prefer to comment on?" "I like to lecture on the Kegon Sutra," he replied. Enkan then asked, "In the Kegon Sutra, how many Dharma worlds are mentioned?" The scholar monk elatedly replied, "Four kinds of Dharma worlds are mentioned in it," and then went on to talk eloquently of Kegon philosophy. Enkan listened silently. When the scholar monk finished talking, Enkan raised a fan he happened to have in his hand and asked, "To which Dharma world does *this* belong?" The scholar monk could not even utter a word in reply. Enkan concluded, "Your knowledge is not of any use, is it? It is like a small lamp under the shining sun. It seems to have no light."

There is another example in *Hekigan-roku* (The Blue Rock Records): Once in China there was an emperor called Bu-tei, who was an earnest Buddhist follower. He invited a famous Zen Master, Fudaishi, to his palace and asked him to give a lecture on the Diamond Prajna Sutra. The emperor and all the noble audience were in the hall waiting to hear Fudaishi's edifying lecture. Fudaishi quietly stepped up to the lectern. With a stick he had in his hand he struck the table in front of him, and then, without a word, stepped down from the platform. The emperor and the audience were aghast, but there was a philosopher in the audience, called Shiko, who declared, "Your Majesty, the lecture on the Diamond Prajna Sutra is over!"

If I could follow the good example of the old Masters and strike the table rather than write this essay on Zen characteristics, it would be a really ideal Zen demonstration. At any rate, Zen Masters always try to help us realize that however great the conceptual knowledge and understanding may be, in the face of real experience concepts are like flakes of snow fallen on a burning fire.

Not relying on letters

The real life and spirit of Zen is an experiential fact. It does not rely on letters, that is, on written or verbal expressions which function within the dualistic limitations. From the very beginnings of human self-consciousness, human beings have been making the mistake of confounding the experiential fact and its expressions in letters, which are just the conceptual shadows of the fact. We are liable to believe that the experience itself exists in letters and words. Zen, which insists that the direct, genuine experience is basic, regards letters and verbal expressions as of secondary importance.

Master Eisai therefore declares from this point of view, "Affirmatively speaking, all the sutras are Zen expressions. Negatively speaking, there is not a word that can be a Zen expression." Here the affirmative standpoint is at the same time the negative standpoint, and both point to nothing else but the Truth itself.

There is a *mondo* recorded in *Dento-roku* (The Transmission of the Lamp): There was once a Zen Master named Sekito (700–790), and many monks came to his place to study under him. Sekito, however, did not give them any lectures at all. Finally the monks could no longer be patient, and one day they forcefully urged the Master to preach. To their surprise, Sekito this time quite easily agreed to do so, and he ordered the monk in charge to ring the bell to announce that a lecture would be given. All the monks assembled in the hall. The Master quietly stepped up to the lectern and said, "For clarification of sutras, there are sutra scholars. For philosophical explanations there are philosophers. I am, however, a Zen Master, and you should well realize it." So saying, he stepped down from the platform and returned to his room.

The monks, of course, asked him to preach because they wished to know the true Zen interpretation of Buddhism. Their teacher Sekito was well aware of what his disciples wanted. Had he so wished, he could have given them a good philosophical interpretation of the Buddhist principles. He was, however, a good Zen Master, and he knew too well how useless this kind of an approach would be. He therefore demonstrated his teaching by his own direct action. For a Zen man there can be no better demonstration of the Truth, and there can be no more cordial instructions. Usually we are too accustomed to logical explanations. However exact and detailed the explanations may be, they are, after all, only going round and round in circles, and never get to the experience itself.

Master Tokusan was a much more severe kind of Zen Master. Once a monk came to see him and, according to the Buddhist manner, made a bow to the Master before asking a question. However, before he had finished bowing, Tokusan gave him a blow of his stick. The monk did not know what it was all about, and said, "I have just bowed to you and have not asked you any question yet. Why have you struck me?" "It is no use to wait till you start talking," was the reply Tokusan gave him. In such a strict denial of words we are to see how earnestly Zen insists on the experience itself.

How could we then come to the direct experience of the fundamental Truth itself? The next two maxims are the answers: Pointing directly to one's Mind, and Attainment of Buddhahood by seeing into one's Nature.

Pointing directly to one's Mind

Here Zen teaches that if we want to experience the Truth, the Reality itself, we must once and for all transcend the blind alley of dualistic human intellect.

Here the word "Mind" (心) is used to represent the Fundamental Absolute Truth. The Mind here does not refer to thought or emotion, nor does it refer to human psychology which is an object of scientific research. It is not the consciousness, nor the psyche which is dealt with by psychiatrists, either. When we go beyond all these, wash them off, and transcend their limitations, for the first time we can reach the Mind which is also called the Buddha Mind, the Absolute Mind, the Spirituality, or the Truth.

"To point direct" means to cast away all fixed ideas and to be one with the Reality, the Truth itself, without any media.

When Zen Master Sekito was still a training monk, one day he went out to a mountain to work with his fellow monks. They came to a narrow mountain path and were prevented from going further by a thicket of vines and creepers. The monk at the head of the group suddenly turned back to Sekito and said, "The creepers are all over and we cannot go any further. Would you lend me the big knife you have?" Sekito unsheathed his big mountain knife, and without a word thrust out the knife with the sharp edge toward him. The companion was frightened, and withdrew his hand crying, "Stop the nonsense! Let me have the hilt!" Sekito's reply was sharper than the edge of the knife. He said, "What is the use of the hilt?" The monk could not utter a word in reply.

We are apt to stick to the hilt which is of secondary importance, and miss the Truth altogether. Sekito is urging us to get hold of the fundamental Truth direct. Here we see the truth of direct pointing.

Attainment of Buddhahood by direct seeing into one's Nature

This is a very important maxim which shows the aim of Zen. First I will give the literal explanation of the phrase.

"Nature" as used here is not something one has acquired after he was born, but it is the "true innate Nature with which one was primarily born." It is the Absolute Nature at the very foundation of existence.

Zen does not say to "know" this absolute fundamental Nature, but it says to "see" into the Nature. This shows a unique characteristic of Zen. The Nature points to the religious Reality which has no form, and Zen uses such a concrete expression "to see," rather than an intellectual expression such as "to know." By doing so, Zen claims that the basis has to be the fact actually experienced by each person, not the knowledge or idea or concept about it.

This religious experience of "seeing into one's Nature" is called *kensho* (見性) in Japanese. By this one attains his religious personality. In Christian terminology, one is saved by God. In Buddhist terminology, it is "to attain to Buddhahood." The fourth maxim can therefore be paraphrased: "By the fact of religious experience one attains his Buddhahood."

The word "Buddha" today is often understood to mean some outside absolute and transcendental being. Here, however, the term Buddha is used in its original Sanskrit meaning, namely, "an enlightened one." It is a common noun that can take a plural form. It does not refer to any almighty absolute being outside ourselves, but to a human being. In *The Song of Zazen* by Hakuin, the term Buddha comes in its first line where he says, "All beings are primarily Buddhas." Here the word is used in the same meaning, and you may read my clarification of the term "Buddha" in that essay.

Now the last two maxims, "Pointing directly to one's Mind," and "Attainment of Buddhahood by seeing into one's Nature," can be summarized: Zen teaches us to go beyond the dualistic discriminations of our ordinary consciousness, and to be directly and actually one with the True Nature. Zen claims that one has to open his spiritual eye to the new vista, and be revived as a new man. This kind of theoretical interpretation, however, is no more than a stuffed lion. It looks like a lion, but it is not a true, living lion any longer. Zen Masters are never tired of pointing directly to one's Mind, that is, they always present to their disciples vivid living religious experiences.

There is a *mondo* in *Dento-roku*. It occured in the Tang dynasty in China while the famous Zen Master Yakusan (750–834) was still a training monk. Once he visited Master Sekito and asked, "I have heard that recently there are people in the south who talk about 'Pointing directly to one's Mind, and the attainment to Buddhahood by seeing into one's Nature.' What could this mean?" Sekito answered, "Neither affirmation nor negation will do. Both miss *It* altogether!" Yakusan was completely at a loss as to how to interpret this reply. When he asked him further, Sekito instructed him to go and see another Master, Baso, in the west. According to this advice, Yakusan made the long journey to see Baso and asked him the same question, to which Baso gave a quite unexpected reply, for he said, "You see, sometimes I raise my eyebrows, and sometimes I goggle my eyes. Sometimes it is good and affirmed, and sometimes it is bad and negated."

Fortunately, Yakusan could see through the Truth by this instruction.

This *mondo* shows us how hard Zen Masters try to take away our discriminating consciousness and intellectual reasoning, which really enslave us. They are genuine Zen Masters who will just point directly to the Absolute Truth, and who try to present the opportunities for their disciples to be awakened to the True Self, direct and concrete. Here again we can see a unique characteristic of Zen.

As you have noticed, I have repeatedly mentioned the casting away, or transcending of dualistic knowledge. This is because in Zen the fact of experience is of vital importance, but I am *not* saying that intellectual approaches are of no significance. Correct understanding and concepts can help promote mutual understanding between people of the East and the West, and can help human beings develop a new culture. But Zen as a religion is purely a religion of human realization, or self-awakening. It teaches us, human beings, to attain *satori* and live a new life in this world as new men of *satori*. It insists that this inner conversion should be carried out by oneself, that one can attain his Zen personality by oneself by searching inwardly, not relying on anything outside. It declares that man has the potentiality for attaining *satori*. This should be happy tidings for human beings.

It is not easy for anyone, however, to cast away the chain of ignorance and discrimination all at once. A very strong will is required, and one has to search single-heartedly for his True Self, within himself. Here, hard training is needed in Zen, and it never resorts to an easy-going, instant means. In the next chapter, therefore, I will discuss "Training in Zen."

TRAINING IN ZEN

Zen is the way of complete self-realization: a living human being who follows the way of Zen can attain *satori* and then live a new life as a Buddha, that is, as an enlightened man. The follower of Zen does not ask for any outside help nor rely on anything other than himself in attaining the ideal Zen personality. Zen is thus based on human nature, and in this sense it is thoroughly rational. On the other hand, because Zen claims that *satori* experience is of the utmost importance, it is sometimes called a mystic religion. Although the word mystic is used, Zen is not mysticism in the ordinary sense because its realization, or awakening experience, is the result of long years of training. Training in Zen is required in order to testify to the Truth of Self Nature.

In the introduction to *Mumonkan* (The Gateless Gate), which is one of the most famous Zen texts, there is a famous phrase: "The Great Tao has no gate. There are infinite ways to reach it." From the primary standpoint of Zen, we do not have to follow the traditional pattern of training in pursuing the way to Zen. The

Great Tao has no gate; there are no fixed rules or procedures to be observed in studying Zen. This is a unique characteristic of Zen. It asks us to come in freely from any direction. There is a relevant story in a Zen text:

Once a young monk called Kyosho came to Zen Master Gensha (831–908) to study under him. Kyosho said, "I have come over here seeking the Truth. Where can I start to get into Zen?" At this Gensha the Master asked Kyosho, "Can you hear the murmuring of the mountain stream?" "Yes, Master, I can hear it," Kyosho replied. "Enter Zen from there!" was the Master's answer. Some time later a lay Zen student, Kyo, told that story to Master An of Sengan and asked, "Because Kyosho answered that he *could* hear the murmuring of the mountain stream when Gensha asked him if he could hear it, Gensha could instruct him to enter Zen from there. If, however, Kyosho had said that he could *not* hear it, how would Master Gensha have instructed him?" An suddenly called out, "Mr. Kyo!" Kyo answered, "Yes Master!" At this the Master said, "Enter Zen from *there*!" See how utterly free the Master was in any circumstances.

Truly, the Great Tao has no gate, and the way to Zen is open everywhere. However, only those who have actually experienced it can

33

declare it. Those who have not awakened to the Truth should not, or cannot, claim an easy agreement with it, for we generally live under a variety of adverse circumstances which prevent us from opening our eyes to the Truth, from having religious experience.

Human beings have developed a highly refined culture in which they live with all sorts of desires. The religious quest, or spiritual inquiry concerning the eternal, is an expression of a noble human desire. This is a uniquely human inquiry, or yearning, basic to man. Once one has this yearning, or spiritual quest, he will naturally try to satisfy it. One possible method of spiritual inquiry is the observance of religious practices.

Zen, especially Rinzai Zen, emphasizes the primary importance of religious experience which will satisfy the human spiritual yearning, and it maintains that the essence of religion lies in religious experience. In the days of the early Zen Masters, there were no fixed training methods, but they naturally went through their own inner spiritual darkness, followed by the moment of religious awakening. They were all real religious geniuses who could attain *satori* by themselves.

Tokusan Sengan (782–865), for example, went through a typical searching and training process at a time when the methods and disciplines of Zen training had not been established. He was a highly educated man, too, and for this reason his searching in Zen presents an interesting example.

Tokusan lived in the northwestern mountain district of China where he carried on academic studies of Buddhism for some time. There he became an authority on the Diamond Sutra and won public recognition for his scholarship. One day he heard that in southern China the Zen Buddhists were becoming influential, talking about "transmission outside the scriptures, and not relying on letters." This could not be approved by scholars. He felt indignant at such teaching. As he was proud and confident of his capability as a Buddhist philosopher, he declared, "I will overthrow the den of Zen devils and exterminate them!" Then this advocator of the Diamond Sutra set forth on his journey to the South, carrying all the notes and records of his long study of the Diamond Sutra.

Somehow a human being cannot be fully satisfied with intellectual knowledge or understanding alone. In the depth of his personality he feels that something is lacking. Such deep inner quest is called true religious inquiry. Tokusan was, in fact, starting to take the first step in his religious training here. In training, the inner urge or quest is necessary.

Tokusan planned first to go to Ryotan in Central China, for a famous Zen Master Soshin lived on a mountain there. When he arrived at the foot of the mountain he found a tea house by the roadside and thought that he might have a snack before climbing the mountain. He ordered it from an old woman at the tea house. Now, snack in the Chinese language is *tenjin* (点心) which means literally "to light up the mind." Apparently this old woman of the tea house was not an ordinary sort of lady. She asked Tokusan, "What do you have in the box on your shoulders?" "O yes," Tokusan replied, "I have a most valuable sutra called the Diamond Sutra in it." At this, the attitude of the old woman changed. "Is that so!" she said, "Then I have a question to ask you. If you can answer my question, I will provide you with a lunch. If, however, you should fail to give me a satisfactory answer, I am sorry but you will have to go without a snack."

Tokusan was a proud and confident scholar. He replied, "All right. You may ask me any question." At this the woman said, "In the Diamond Sutra it is written that 'Past mind is unattainable; present mind is unattainable; and future mind is unattainable.' You say you are going to light up your mind. Which mind, now, are you going to light up?" Tokusan was unable to answer the old woman's question.

"The Three Minds Unattainable" is a famous passage in the Diamond Sutra in which the *satori* experience is taken up in relation to time. In other words, religious time, or the inner time, as against physical time is discussed here. As a capable scholar, Tokusan could well have explained the unattainability of the three minds from the intellectual or philosophical point of view. The old woman here, however, was not asking for a logical explanation *about* it. She wanted to see the truth of "The Three Minds Unattainable" in the actual fact of taking a meal. The questioner was definitely asking the question from a different perspective.

From the viewpoint of Zen training, the old woman's question served to awaken Tokusan's religious inquiry, or spiritual quest, which had been growing within him unnoticed. Earnest human pursuit of happiness is not always directed outwardly to the scientific field. It can be directed inwardly and be such a significant religious inquiry.

Tokusan had to admit his inability to give the answer and at the suggestion of the old woman of the tea house he determined to study

Zen under Master Ryotan. It is not known how long he studied under Ryotan, or what sort of inner searching process he went through. Certainly, however, his spiritual quest aroused within himself must have driven him to the last extremity. I understand that in the West there is a saying: "Man's extremity is God's opportunity." Tokusan must have been at his very extremity.

One day Master Ryotan and Tokusan were spending the evening together. Ryotan said, "It is getting dark. You had better return to your place." Tokusan said "Good night" to the Master, and stepped outside. He returned to the Master, however, saying, "It is so dark outside." Then the Master lit a candle to give to Tokusan and just as Tokusan held out his hand and was about to get hold of the candle, Ryotan vehemently blew out the flame. At this moment, all of a sudden Tokusan was awakened. The chronicle just records that "He was awakened, and made a bow to the Master."

At the extremity of no-mind, no-self, where neither heaven nor earth exists, all of a sudden the moment of breaking through this no-mind was given. He was revived as the Great Self of no-self. Reviving in Zen means this inner awakening experience. Traditionally it is called *kensho*, or more simply, *satori*. It is also called the opening of the spiritual eye, or the discovery of the True Self.

Tokusan was no longer the scholar monk he had been up to the day before. The next morning he threw out all his notes and records of the Diamond Sutra which he had brought with him, burning them in front of the monastery. He declared, "Any knowledge or learning is just like a drop of water fallen in a valley when it is compared with the depth of experience." The sutra commentator Tokusan was revived as a Zen Man Tokusan.

Zen history tells us that Masters in the early days all came to the attainment of their *satori* by themselves by going through a natural and unique training process of their own. If we, however, try to summarize the processes of these Masters' spiritual development, we can find more or less similar patterns. Tokusan's case is a typical example. Namely, they first start with an extremely intense religious quest; then comes hard, strong-willed search and discipline, which will be followed by spiritual crises, or a sense of the abyss; and finally, they experience the moment of awakening. These are the inner processes they generally go through.

Zen training originally followed individual and natural courses of development. Our

ordinary life, however, is so complex that it is
not possible for everyone of us to go through
such an inner natural process of religious
searching as the old great Masters did. Zen
Masters wished to help students in future
generations in their search for the Truth. Out
of their compassion they reflected on their own
training days and tried to find some helpful
means for their fellow beings. Thus, as time
went on, a pattern of Zen training as we have it
today came to be established.

Zen monasteries in Japan are all institutions
where Zen training thus established is actually
being carried on. In any monastery, the following three conditions are particularly required of
a training monk as indispensable requisites in
Zen training:

*1. To have a firm faith and commitment in under-
taking one's training. (大信根)*

*2. To have a strong will to carry on under hard
discipline. (大精進)*

*3. To have the Great Doubt—Spiritual Quest—
which will be the prajna (true wisdom) basis in
searching for the Truth. (大疑団)*

If any of the three is lacking, it is impossible
for the monk to accomplish his Zen training;
when these three requisites are present, day and

40

night, he will be encouraged to carry on his discipline.

Under such spiritual conditions, monks go on with their training, practicing *zazen* (Zen meditation) and taking *sanzen* (personal Zen interview). In Zen, we have Soto Zen and Rinzai Zen, and their ways and methods of training are somewhat different. As I am a Rinzai Zen Master, here I am discussing Zen training in Rinzai.

Regularly in the morning and evening for several hours every day monks practice *zazen*, but they also engage in all sorts of work in day-time since a monastery is self-supporting.

Once in every month they have a special training period, of a week's duration, which is called *sesshin* in Japanese. During this *sesshin* period they exclusively do *zazen*. In addition to these regular monthly *sesshin*, at the beginning of December they have a special, most inten-sive training period to commemorate Sakya-muni Buddha's attainment of *satori*. At this greatest *sesshin*, a week is regarded as a day, that is, they just keep on doing *zazen* through a week's time without going to bed, although they are allowed to sleep in the sitting posture for a few hours at night.

Such hard *zazen* practice does not mean just to assume a quiet, full-lotus sitting posture. In addition to stopping physical movements, one is required to cast away all thoughts and consciousness of himself. He has to be actually in the state of no-thought, no-mind, and no-form, where there is neither the self that is sitting, nor the earth which is supporting him.

Old Zen Masters described such a state of no-thought and said, "Sheer darkness all over," or, "To be confined to an ice cave ten thousand miles thick." In other words, one is to be the True Self, or the true genuine absolute subjectivity that can no longer be objectified.

It may be easy to talk about somebody else's hard training and to describe his psychological development in training. It is most difficult, however, for anybody to actually go through such training. One has to be prepared to risk his life, and even then *satori* may not be accessible. Zen has been, therefore, described from olden days as the way for only a handful of geniuses.

Hakuin, the author of *The Song of Zazen*, was a Zen Master who had once had hard training days himself. He says it is like a mountain climber who has lost his footing while scaling a steep cliff. His life now hangs on a single vine to which he clings with all his might. Hakuin demands that he let go of the vine. In other words, he tells him to die once.

42

When Zen talks of no-mind or no-self, it does not refer to an idea nor engage in conceptual speculation. No-mind has to be experienced by each individual as an actual fact. It cannot be just easily accomplished. If one hesitates in his search because it is so difficult, then the time will never come for him to open his spiritual eye to a new world. At a monastery, therefore, a kind of artificial training method is used to encourage training monks: *koan* and *sanzen* are used.

Without going into a detailed explanation of the *koan*, they may be briefly described as sayings left by Zen Masters to show their own Zen experience. These sayings and phrases sound so irrational that our ordinary dualistic reasoning utterly fails to interpret them. For instance, they say:

"If you clap both your hands there is a sound; what is the sound of one hand clapping?"
"See your Self before you were born!" or
"Before Abraham I am" can be a Zen *koan*.

This very irrationality of *koan*, which refuses all the intellectual approaches, plays a most important role in Zen training, for it makes us realize the limitations of our discriminating intellect and finally drives us to despair of it.

After a novice has exerted himself to learn

43

how to sit in the full-lotus posture for a certain period of time, the Zen Master at a monastery will give him a *koan* and the novice will do *zazen* with the *koan*, which will drive him to despair of his knowledge and intellect until he will come to have the real Great Doubt, or Spiritual Quest. Zen training seeks to cast away all discriminating consciousness. This process of casting away one's discriminating consciousness is not at all easy, in practice. Therefore, at the monastery they take *sanzen* to help Zen studies.

Sanzen is a personal Zen interview with a Zen Master. The training monks go one by one into the Master's room, each approaching him in a traditional manner which must be strictly observed, and sits face to face with the Master, and presents the results of his discipline. It is a most serious occasion for the novice who is required to reveal all his Zen ability and spiritual insight to the Master. The outcome of his Zen training which he presents is not a conceptual conclusion, nor a result of reasoning or speculation: it must be the spirituality, or Zen attaining, he has reached by *zazen* and *koan*. It is natual, therefore, that a monk cannot be ready all the time to take *sanzen* in a satisfactory manner.

Even so, this *sanzen* takes place several times a day at the monastery during the *sesshin*, the intensive training period, and two or three times a day even on ordinary days. It can be easily imagined how difficult it is for the training monk. If a novice is not ready to take *sanzen* at all, several senior monks in the Zen Hall will forcefully drag him out and chase him to the room of the Master. The Master will spurn him and drive him out. Every day a novice has to go through such hard discipline. By encouragement given, and by his strong spiritual quest, his inner search is intensified. He puts his heart and soul into his training. He comes to the extremity where no logic and no verbalisms are of any avail. His eyes are open, yet he is not conscious of seeing. He has ears, but is not conscious of hearing. He is actually in the state of no-mind, no-thought, where there is neither the self nor the world.

Rinzai said, "Years ago when I was not awakened to the Truth, it was sheer darkness all over." He was in the abyss of unconsciousness before attaining *satori*.

When one is in such a condition, it is not unusual for all sorts of abnormal, morbid psychological phenomena and illusions to appear. From olden days, however, Masters have strongly warned us not to be attached to them, but to throw them away.

How long the dark night of unconsciousness will continue cannot be foreseen. It depends on each individual. All of a sudden, however, and quite unexpectedly, the moment of awakening comes to the monk. When this blessed moment is given, the abyss of unconsciousness is broken through.

Years ago, Zen Master Reiun, after thirty years of hard discipline, had this blessed moment of awakening when he saw a peach blossom in bloom. The unconscious self of Reiun revived as the True Self. Reiun was born anew in the world. He was the peach, and the universe was full of its fragrance; or rather, he was the universe itself now.

Master Kyogen, after a long search, came to the moment of awakening when he heard the sound of a stone hitting a bamboo. Here he was resounding throughout the universe as the rap of the stone.

A Japanese Zen Master in the Tokugawa period named Shido Bunan had a *waka* poem:

Die while alive, and be completely dead,
Then do whatever you will, all is good.

The aim of Zen training is to die while alive, that is, to actually become the self of no-mind, and no-form, and then to revive as the True Self of no-mind and no-form. In Zen training, therefore, what is most important is for one to revive from the abyss of unconsciousness. Zen training is *not* the emotional process of just being in the state of oneness, nor is it just to have the "feeling" of no-mind. *Prajna* wisdom (true wisdom) has to shine out after breaking through the extremity of the Great Doubt, and then still further training is needed so that one can freely live the Zen life and work in the world as a new man. At any rate, such deep spiritual experience has a great significance which we should not ignore in developing the spiritual culture of mankind today and in the future.

Hard training is carried on at Zen monasteries today with the purpose of reproducing in a novice the similar inner processes the old Zen Masters experienced. We have to be careful and serious in strictly and correctly adopting the training methods used.

In studying Zen, therefore, those who want to appreciate it as a cultural value, or as religious philosophy, can very well do so from such perspectives. Those, however, who want to experience it in themselves should be prepared to go through the hardship, and should never be tempted to follow an easy shortcut. Recently there have been people who talk about instant enlightenment, or those who take drugs in an attempt to experience *satori*. Whatever claims they may make, I declare that such approaches are not authentic, true Zen at all.

I should like to add a few last words here. True as it may be that Zen is really a supreme way to the Truth, it is obvious that not everyone can be expected to have the training required for attainment of the exquisite moment of *satori*. We have to admit that basic Zen is a very difficult way and only a handful of religiously endowed people under favourable conditions can attain *satori*.

There has to be another way of Zen open for ordinary people to follow even though it may be a secondary approach. In this way people can learn the teachings of old Zen Masters and can make the religious living attitudes of the old Masters the guiding principles of their lives. Thus they can try to follow the examples of Zen life as much as possible under the circumstances in which they live. This might be called the Zen life based on faith. I should like to discuss in more detail this Zen life for ordinary people, but will have to leave it to some other occasion.

ZEN PERSONALITY

Zen is not a conceptual conclusion reached by speculation and reasoning. The way of Zen cannot be found by our ordinary dualistic knowledge. Not only that, but all the knowledge and thoughts which are products of our ordinary consciousness are to be completely cast away. When this is done, there is the fact of actual experience, where one is awakened to no-mind, or so-called "Nothingness." Zen is found in this inner experience.

Objectively speaking, therefore, Zen experience is to come to the realization of the very foundation of existence. Subjectively speaking, Zen can be explained as the awakening to the innermost spirituality of mankind. In Zen we use a simple word *satori*, which is often translated "Enlightenment," to refer to the fact of religious experience.

We are, however, liable to confuse such absolute spirituality with some of our ordinary and psychological experience. This is because whenever an attempt is made to express this new vista experienced in Zen *satori*, in our culture the expression will go through the process of abstraction and conceptualization and will have its own existence apart from the fact of the experience itself. An expression is born of the fact of experience, and an experience gives birth to thought. Of course thoughts have their own cultural value and significance. But if the experience is forgotten and Zen is talked about at the level of its expression alone, then Zen itself is already dead, and what is talked about is its lifeless shadow.

For instance, the Sixth Patriarch, Eno (Hui-neng in Chinese, 638–713), gave a conceptual description of Zen based on his Zen experience, "In our teaching, no-thought is the principle, no-form is the foundation, and no-abode is the basis." For Eno, no-thought, no-form, no-abode, was not just an idea or reasoning, nor was it a conceptual truth, but it was the concrete fact. This means that Eno was a personality of no-thought, no-form, and of no-abode. Here the expression is returned to the experience, and it operates as a living personality.

We, however, have the unfortunate tendency of failing to see clearly through the fact. Zen Masters were well aware of this human weakness and tried their best to open our experiential spiritual eyes. As one of these efforts they emphasized the necessity of realizing the personality that is characteristic of Zen experience, so the students would have concrete, firm experiences of their own. In a sense, Zen can be interpreted as the hard process of returning thoughts and expressions to the original experiential facts from which those thoughts and expressions originated.

One day a monk asked Zen Master Joshu (778–897), "What is *dhyana*?" Joshu gave a quite unexpected reply, for he said, "It is non-*dhyana*." The monk asked again, "How can *dhyana* be non-*dhyana*?" Joshu did not give any theoretical explanations to the monk's "How?" but said, "It's alive! It's alive!"

The dychotomy or contradiction of *dhyana* and non-*dhyana* only exists in the world of discriminating logic, for "the alive" goes beyond the contradiction of *dhyana* and non-*dhyana*. "The alive," which is the personality of *satori*, knows no such contradiction.

A good Zen Master always works like this. He urges his disciple to have an eye to see through the relativistic oppositions and contradictions, and makes him grasp the opportunity in himself of making a leap.

Zen personality should not be interpreted as a psychological ego. It cannot be an idea or knowledge based on dualistic, discriminating logic, either. When all these are wiped away,

51

the personality with the form of no-form will present itself. Then Zen is alive here in this personality. In Zen such personality is called the "Primary Man," for such a man cannot be produced by human efforts. Such a man is also called "The Master." This means he is the absolute basic subjectivity. In order to avoid any fixed idea, sometimes such unusual expressions as "This" or "It" are used as well.

The Zen Master Zuigan Shigen (ca. 900) has this *mondo*: Every day Master Zuigan would call out to himself, "Hey, Master!" and he would answer to himself, "Yes." Then he would ask himself, "Are you awakened?" and would again answer himself, "Yes, I am." Then he would go on to say, "Don't be careless and be deceived by others!" "Oh, no, I will not," he would answer himself. (*Mumonkan* Case 12)

What kind of man could this Master be, to whom Zuigan addressed himself every day? Did he not speak to the absolute subjective personality which was within himself, yet transcended his small self? This "personality" must go beyond the individualistic ego, even though it embraces it within. This *mondo* was his kind and direct advice and teaching in order that we should be awakened to "It" or "This" which has been lost and forgotten in us. For those who have not had the experience of having their Zen eyes opened, and who consequently live by ordinary, dualistic logic, such actions may seem nonsensical. But now I should like to ask you to consider another *mondo*.

A monk who had been studying under Master Zuigan came to another Master, Gensha (831–908). Gensha asked the newcomer, "Where have you been recently?" "I was with Zuigan," the monk replied. "In what manner does Zuigan instruct his disciples?" Gensha asked. The monk told him how Zuigan would every day call out to himself, "Oh Master," and would answer himself. Gensha listened quietly to the story and then remarked, "I see, it is rather interesting," and he asked the monk again, "Why didn't you stay with Zuigan longer?" The monk said, "He has passed away." At this reply, Master Gensha asked a very unexpected question, "If you call out to him now, 'Oh Master,' as he used to do, will he reply?" It is recorded that the monk was silent. He was unable to say anything.

Gensha asked, "If we call out to Zuigan now, who is already dead, 'Oh Master!' will he answer?" What can it be that Gensha is seeing here? What does he want to tell us by this? Unfortunately the spiritual eye of the monk was not opened. He failed to see through Zuigan's spirituality, or Gensha's. Or, we can say that if he had seen through Zuigan's Truth, he should have been able to see the Truth of Gensha, and the Truth of his own self which is the "Master," too. I should like to stress here the necessity of getting hold of the "alive" personality in Zen experience.

People generally, however, try to understand the Zen personality with their yardstick of dualistic knowledge. This Zen personality belongs to the sphere where any consciousness or discrimination has not yet started to move. It does not belong to the world of ordinary consciousness. It was therefore quite natural that the monk could not utter a word in reply to the question, "If you would call out now to him, 'Oh Master!' would he answer?"

In one way or another, human beings have to once and for all make a leap out of this discriminating consciousness. As long as they remain in the dualistic world their sufferings will never be dispersed, nor will their contradictions be solved. In other words, they will be unable to have the Zen personality. If we want real freedom and true emancipation, we must at any cost make this transcendental leap. Zen instructions in this regard are uniquely direct and appropriate.

Master Rinzai (d. 867) was the most representative figure in this regard in the history of

Zen, for he kept on emphasizing Zen personality, or the personality which is characteristic of Zen experience, all through his life. The following passage from his sermons is most famous: "Over a mass of reddish flesh there sits a True Man who has no title. He is all the time coming in and out from your own sense-organs. If you have not yet testified to the fact, look! Look!" A monk came out and asked, "What is this True Man of no title?" Rinzai came down from the platform, took hold of the monk's cloak, and demanded, "Speak! Speak!" The monk hesitated. Rinzai, releasing him, said, "The True Man of no title, what a dirty thing it is!" Then he returned to his room.

We have, in Zen, such an extraordinary direct and strict way of training the monks, and we feel deeply impressed when we come across it. Let me, for emphasis, repeat this famous *mondo* here.

One day Rinzai appeared on the platform to give a Zen talk. He addressed his disciples almost scoldingly, "Over this actual physical body of yours there is an absolutely free Man who goes beyond all the limitations. He is alive and actively working from morning till night whether you are asleep or awake, through your sense-organs. Now, those of you who have not yet seen through this Man, see and get hold of

55

him!" A monk stepped forward out of the congregation and asked, "What is this True Man of no title?" Master Rinzai, however, did not give him even a word of explanation, logical or conceptual, but stepped down from the platform, seized the monk by the coat, and urged him, to the contrary, to give the answer, and demanded, "Speak! Speak!"

What a direct and vivid instruction this is! He did not resort to any kind of explanation at all, but demonstrated himself in front of the questioner as the living True Man of no title. The inner eye of the questioning monk was not opened yet, however, and he did not have sufficient Zen ability to see through the Zen personality so clearly presented in front of him. He could only stand aghast, not knowing how to react. At the next moment, Rinzai thrust off the monk. "How dirty and disgusting this True Man of no title is!" So saying, he immediately returned to his room.

A man whose Zen eye was clearly opened would have seen the True Man of no title vividly working in this last demonstration of Rinzai. Dr. Daisetz T. Suzuki said in his book entitled "*Rinzai no Kihon Shiso*" (Basic Characteristics of Rinzai) that "The whole Zen thought developed in *Rinzai-roku* (Records of Lin-chi) is based on and revolving around this one word

'Man'—that is, the Zen personality."

Buddha Nature, or True Mind, as used in Zen, is not an idea nor is it a concept. It is not something considered to be potential in us, nor is it something that is supposed to be immanent in us. But it is the most concrete, actual fact which should be grasped about our physical body here and now. The uniqueness of Zen can be seen here. Zen Masters point to it, and try their best to somehow make their disciples firmly get hold of it.

Although the True Man of no title has a definite and concrete personality, he will not be restricted by the physical body of five or six feet high, nor will he be limited in time to the life of sixty or seventy years. He is an absolute being. Dr. Suzuki stated, in describing such a personality, "He is individualistic, yet he is transcending the individuality. He is transcendental, still he is an individual." Thus Dr. Suzuki had to use the expression of "self-identity of contradiction," which goes beyond logic. However clearly expressed it may be, if it remains a logical statement it ceases to be a living fact in itself.

When Rinzai came down from the platform and demanded, "Speak! Speak!" we are able to see here a living personality vividly at work. Again, when he thrust away the monk, saying,

"What a dirty thing this True Man of no title is!" and returned to his room, we are able to appreciate the fine example of a Zen personality vividly and clearly represented.

About one hundred years before the time of Rinzai, there was a Zen Master called Sekito Kisen (700–790). One day one of his disciples, Dogo Enchi (769–835), who later became a Master, asked, "What is the essence of Zen?" Sekito replied, "Unattainable and unknowable." Dogo continued, "Is there anything more to it?" Sekito's reply this time was, "How clear and vast the sky is! There is nothing to disturb the white cloud floating." Dogo asked about the ultimate truth of Zen. When his teacher replied negatively, "Unattainable and unknowable," Dogo was somehow not convinced, and had to ask again, "Is there anything more to it?" He interpreted the Master's reply, "Unattainable and unknowable" only literally, and his mind eye to see the living truth out of this seemingly conceptual reply was not yet opened. Sekito, at this second question of Dogo, "Is there anything more than that?" said, "How clear and vast the sky is! Nothing to disturb the white cloud floating!" Superficially interpreted, while the first reply, "Unattainable and unknowable," was a static answer, Sekito this time gave an active reply.

Is such interpretation, however, correct?

The essence of Buddhism is in the real, living personality. If we fail to see it, all the interpretations are just logical products in the world of dualism. Both the negative expression of "unattainable and unknowable!" and the freedom of the white cloud floating are two working aspects naturally flowing out of an absolute Zen personality. They are in fact neither static nor active. Two are one, and one is two. If we fail to see this through, we are unable to talk with Sekito.

A Zen Master Ungan Donsei (780–841) was a close friend of Dogo, the same Dogo who questioned Sekito. Ungan has the following *mondo* on the subject of Zen personality. One day Ungan was making tea. Dogo happened to come along and asked, "For whom are you making tea?" Ungan replied, "There is a man who wants to drink tea." "Why, then, don't you make *that* man make tea himself?" Dogo went on to ask. Ungan nonchalantly said, "Well, I happen to be here." Dogo was satisfied at this reply and went away.

Logically speaking, Ungan's remark that "There is a man who wants to drink tea," will naturally be interpreted to refer to another fellow who wants tea, apart from the speaker Ungan himself. Actually, however, there is just

59

one Ungan here. A man here, therefore, should mean the transcendental absolute personality— Zen personality—who is with Ungan, or is in Ungan. Dogo, of course, was well aware of it. Although Dogo clearly appreciated Ungan's Zen spirituality in his first reply, he went on to test further how deep and true his Zen attainment was.

In his second question, "Why don't you make *that* man make tea himself?" Dogo purposely took the standpoint of the individual self. Ungan's Zen attainment was, however, so firm that it was not to be shaken at all. The transcendental self should work as an individual self, too, otherwise it will lose its significance and truth as the transcendental self. Ungan acted as an individual self here, and said, "Well, I happen to be here!" The individual self, who happens to be here, is at the same time the transcendental self who wants to drink tea. It is the Zen personality that is neither two nor one. Dogo and Ungan had a vivid *mondo* on "the alive" in which they demonstrated their actual, concrete, alive Zen personalities. In Zen, between a Master and his disciple, or between fellow disciples, *mondo* is exchanged and they test or train each other's Zen attainment, or inner spirituality in such direct and dynamic ways. This may be a unique method in Zen.

In conclusion, I should like to refer to *Zazen Wasan* (The Song of Zazen), written by Hakuin. For the original song and my comments on its meaning and structure, I leave it to you to read my essay on that subject. Here, I will call your attention to two lines from the song which are related to the subject of this essay. Hakuin's song, which consists of forty-four lines, is an outline of Zen. The song starts with the first line, "All beings are primarily Buddhas," and ends with the forty-fourth line which says, "This person is the body of Buddha." This structure of the song may have many other implications, but more than anything else it shows the fact that Hakuin also stressed the personality which is characteristic of Zen experience, and the necessity of actually attaining this personality.

Needless to say, the first line shows the principle of characteristic Zen teaching, which is based on the Zen view of man. Here, too, the personality which is characteristic of Zen experience can be seen as a principle. When it comes to the last line, the conclusion, this characteristic is more clearly presented, for here we see the real living Man.

Now the Zen personality, which is an individual self and at the same time the transcendental self, is working in this physical body of ours as a vividly living man. He is utterly free, like a white cloud floating in the sky. Where, then, will he live with such freedom? Nowhere else but this place here—this dualistic world of ours.

When such a Zen personality lives in this world, he naturally creates and develops special ethics, expressed in conduct. This, however, presents another subject too great to be discussed here and I will leave it to some other occasion.

ZAZEN WASAN
FOREWORD

Zazen Wasan, "The Song of Zazen," is one of the many writings left by Zen Master Hakuin, a brilliant figure in the Zen history of Japan. Simply written for the common people to give them an outline of Zen, it is widely read, not only by people belonging to Zen organizations, but also by those interested in Zen, and is generally very popular. Because it is in a rhyming verse form, and the expressions used are simple and direct, it is good for chanting as well.

Before going into *Zazen Wasan* with you, I should like to make a few introductory remarks: "Zen" is not to be understood as identical with the Zen School of Buddhism. The term "Zen Buddhism" is generally used to mean a school of Buddhism based on Zen and teaching Zen, an established religion treated as a social organization comparable to other religious sects and schools. "Zen," however, is one of the basic components characterizing Oriental thought, and as such has great influence not only in religion but on various phases of culture. It develops our ideas, and builds our characters. It is wisdom based on religious experience directly connected with the very source of our existence.

63

Zen thus offers its unique significance to our life independent of the religious school called Zen Buddhism.

In this regard, although I am a Zen monk of the Zen School of Buddhism, I sincerely desire that people have a better understanding of "Zen." By introducing *Zazen Wasan* I wish to further the understanding of true Zen which will eventually lead to the peace and happiness of humankind, however long it may take.

ZAZEN WASAN
The Song of Zazen by Hakuin

All beings are primarily Buddhas.   1
Like water and ice,
There is no ice apart from water;
There are no Buddhas apart from beings.

Not knowing how close the Truth is to them, 5
Beings seek for it afar—what a pity!
It is like those who being in water
Cry out for water, feeling thirst.
It is like the rich man's son,
Who has lost his way among the poor.   10

The reason why beings transmigrate
    through the six worlds,
Is because they are lost in the darkness of
    ignorance.
Wandering from darkness to darkness,
How can they ever be free from
    birth-and-death?

As to Zazen taught in the Mahayana,   15
No amount of praise can exhaust its merits.

The Six Paramitas, beginning with
    the Giving,
Observing the Precepts and other good
    deeds, variously enumerated,
As Nembutsu, Repentance, and so on—
All are finally reducible to Zazen.   20

The merit of even a single sitting in Zazen
Erases the countless sins accumulated
    in the past.
Where then are there the evil paths to
    misguide us?
The Pure Land cannot be far away.

Those who, even once, in all humility,   25
Listen to this Truth.
Praise it and faithfully follow it,
Will be endowed with innumerable merits.

But if you turn your eyes within yourselves
And testify to the truth of Self-nature—   30
The Self-nature that is no-nature,
You will have gone beyond the ken of
    sophistry.

The gate of the oneness of cause and effect
    is opened;
The path of non-duality and non-trinity
    runs straight ahead.

Your form being the form of no-form,   35
Your going-and-returning takes place
    nowhere but where you are;
Your thought being the thought of
    no-thought,
Your singing-and-dancing is none other than
    the voice of Dharma.

How boundless and free is the sky of
    Samadhi!
How refreshingly bright, the moon of the   40
    Fourfold Wisdom!

At this moment what is there that you lack!
Nirvana presents itself before you,
Where you stand is the Land of Purity.
Your person, the body of Buddha.

THE BACKGROUND

Zen Master Hakuin

Hakuin, the author of this Song of Zazen, lived from 1685 to 1768. When we think of the average span of man's life in those days in Japan, we can say that 83 years was indeed a long life. The 200th anniversary of Hakuin's death happensd to fall in 1967.

Hakuin was born the third son in the Nagasawa family in a village called Hara, Shizuoka, where beautiful Mt. Fuji, the symbol of Japan, is close by. His father was the station master of the village. The station master in those days was in charge of postal and transportation work.

In his childhood, Hakuin was called Iwajiro. He is said to have had big round shining eyes, and a strong-willed sturdy appearance. In disposition, Iwajiro was said to be bold, courageous and quick in decision. At eleven, he heard a story told by a travelling preacher who had come to the village. According to this story, sinful people who died would definitely go to hell and put through all sorts of torture. Iwajiro was deeply impressed by this. His inner religious aspiration was first awakened around this time.

At fifteen, with the consent of his parents, Iwajiro entered a Zen temple in a village called Shoinji, and was ordained a Zen monk under Master Tanrei. First he followed the usual course of a young Buddhist monk, and pursued his academic studies on Buddhism, visiting learned scholars at various places.

When he was twenty years old, however, studying under Master Bawo, he read that long ago Jimyo, the Zen Master, used to Practice Zazen with a gimlet nearby to punish sleepiness, and thus sought for the True Self. This story moved and inspired Hakuin, who from that time started to devote himself to Zazen singleheartedly, searching for inner light. The way to Enlightenment, however, was steep and difficult, and not easily attainable.

At twenty-four, he was at Eigenji in Takada, Echigo. His training had advanced to the spirituality of Oneness—the identity of subject and object. One day in January, as he was sitting as usual throughout the night in Zazen *samadhi*, the bronze temple bell sounded to announce dawn. At this moment, all of a sudden, he had his awakening. It is recorded that he jumped up with joy.

He was now self-confident. However, soon after this, he met Sogaku and this Zen friend took Hakuin to Zen Master Shoju. For over seven months he stayed close to Shoju, an extremely severe and strict teacher, and under him Hakuin's attainment was further refined and deepened. Hakuin was given the Dharma sanction by Shoju. For ten years after his Enlightenment experience, Hakuin indefatigably kept on with his discipline. Sometimes he went on training journeys on foot to refine his attainment; sometimes he stayed in small mountain retreats to deepen his spirituality.

His unique spiritual power, which, in the latter half of his life unfolded itself in his great religious activities, was all cultivated and prepared during these ten years of discipline after Enlightenment.

When Hakuin was thirty-three years old, a servant came all the way from his parents' home to his mountain retreat to tell him of his father's aged condition, and urged him to return home. Yielding to his persuasion, Hakuin returned home to tend to his father. He moved into Shoinji, which was abandoned with no resident priest to take care of it. Hakuin's religious work for society started henceforth. For approximately the next fifty years, he was active in the training of young monks, in writing, and in preaching to the populace. When he passed away he did so having accomplished great work of historical significance for posterity. We express our admiration for the greatness of Hakuin today in Japan by praising him as: "The greatest sage in 500 years," and "The patriarch who revived Zen."

"The greatest sage in 500 years" means that Hakuin was the kind of great man who appears in this world only once in 500 years. The second phrase, "The patriarch who revived Zen," may need some explanation. Zen was introduced into Japan from China in the Kamakura period (around 1190), and was for the most part accepted by the *samurai*, the ruling class of the country in those days. It gradually took root in the land as a new religion well suited to the age. Later Zen began flourishing in Japan, greatly influencing Japanese culture. In the course of the several hundred years of Zen history, however, the "genuineness of the experience" which comprises the real life and spirit of Zen, gradually declined.

Zen declares itself to be "outside all scriptures and not dependent on letters." This means that the essence of Zen is the fact of its religious experience, i.e., the experience of *satori*. From the Zen viewpoint, all literary expressions or cultural activities are of secondary importance, naturally flowing out from the fact of deep religious experience to take their own forms and expressions. The experience, however, is so personal that it cannot be fully communicated or transmitted to others as can be the resulting cultural expressions or activities. I believe this should be true with any religion. Because of this highly personal quality of Enlightenment experience, the inevitable tendency as time goes on is that the cultural side of Zen may make remarkable progress, while its core, the experiential side declines.

By the time Hakuin was born, although the social functions of Zen organizations in Japan had become quite superficially active and its cultural influence had been noticeable, the inner life of Zen based on direct experience was dying out. Zen in Japan was in a critical situation. Hakuin, a religious genius, was born into this historical situation. Well aware of this crisis in Zen, he devoted his life to reviving the real experiential life of Zen. He trained and left many good disciples, created a new trend in Zen circles which emphasized the vital importance of Enlightenment experience, and aroused an interest in the value of actual practice and training. In fact, Zen history in Japan was changed by Hakuin's efforts, and most of the Rinzai School of Zen teachers in Japan today follow in Hakuin's footsteps. He is thus admired as "The patriarch who revived Zen," or the Dharma Reviver.

Hakuin made every effort to promote true Zen training and Enlightenment experience. It is well known that apart from the traditional *koan* originated in the Sung dynasty, he created new unique *koan* like "Listen to the sound of one hand clapping," in order to help awaken the Zen consciousness of his disciples, and to lead them to definite and thorough-going Enlightenment experience. He also wrote many books to emphasize this point, propagating the teaching of Zen. *Zasen Wasan* is one of these attempts.

As a part of his propagating activities, he made full use of his artistic genius and left many works of calligraphy, as well as a sort of free style painting on which he wrote various Zen verses and lines commenting on the paintings. These paintings of Hakuin are among those that are known as "Zen paintings." They are admired as masterpieces of Zen art, and are valuable cultural treasures of Japan. His paintings and calligraphy strongly appeal directly to the eye and heart with unusual strength and inspiration that seems to emanate from the work. Apart from their great artistic appeal, his comments added to the paintings often well express the spirit of Zen. They are not mere moral teachings or humorous remarks, but point directly to the fact of religious experience of Zen Enlightenment, and illustrate Zen spirituality.

73

For example, in a few simple lines he drew a beautifully formed Mt. Fuji, and as the panegyric on it, he wrote a verse which on the surface sounds like a popular and humorous love song. It says, "My sweetheart is dear Fuji, sitting on the clouds. How I long to see her snow white skin!" From the village where Hakuin spent most of his long life, he could see Mt. Fuji everyday. The view of this gracefully shaped mountain soaring in the blue sky, crowned with pure, white snow, is extremely beautiful. It appears divinely graceful and holy. This holy looking mountain, however, tends to be covered with clouds. In some seasons it is not easy to have a full view of its beauty. Hakuin took this sacred mountain, revered by everybody, as a symbol of the absoluteness of Zen mind and the importance of Zen training.

If one reads these lines lightly, it may sound like only an affectionate ditty: "Fuji is my sweetheart, but she has put on a robe of clouds. How I wish to take off her robe and see her white skin!" If we realize, however, that this sweetheart means Buddha Nature, Suchness, or the One Truth which transcends everything and leads us to fundamental emancipation, its meaning changes. The robe of clouds symbolizes our dualistic feelings of all kinds which cover our eyes and keep us from seeing the Truth. Hakuin,

here, asks us to cast away all the clouds of ignorance, attachment, illusion and return to our
stark naked True Self. In other words, he is
urging us to take hold of our "Original True
Self," with all of our heart and soul, for this experience is the very life and spirit of Zen.

Another example of Hakuin's art is a sort
of cartoon depicting a one-eyed monster and a
blindman. A grotesque-looking monster with
one big headlight-like eye on its forehead, is
fiercely glaring at a blindman who is looking up,
quite unconcernedly and boldly. Hakuin's lines
read, "Hey, I am a one-eyed monster. Aren't
you afraid?" "Why should I be afraid of one-
eye? I have no eyes. It is you that should be
scared of me."

Again, if you glance lightly at the picture,
you may think that it is just a humorous cartoon
with no special significance, and laugh it away.
Yet, what is Hakuin trying to warn us by this?
Are some of us not offending others by our self-
conceit in thinking that we are the elites of the
world because our spiritual eyes are opened to the
Truth? Are we not, without knowing it, embar-
rassing people around us by being bogged in
petty complacency?

Zen always tells us to transcend the dualistic world and open our eyes to the absolute
realm of Oneness. There may be some who

have managed to cast away the dualistic world, but then they contract another kind of disease— that of sticking to Oneness and again losing their freedom. These are the ones to be called the "One-eyed monsters."

We must not allow ourselves to be overwhelmed and enslaved by the brilliant development of scientific civilization which is based on dualism. But at the same time, we should not remain smug in the depths of a non-dualistic spiritual civilization. In order to be the real master of all these, once and for all, we have to cast away even this absolute realm of Oneness and deepen our spirituality until we can say, "Why should I be afraid of One Eye? I have no eyes!" The essence of Zen can be really appreciated when one comes to this point.

In an old Zen text there is a famous *mondo*. One day a monk said to Zen Master Joshu: "I have cast away everything, and there is nothing at all left in my mind. What would you say to that?" To this Joshu gave the unexpected reply: "Cast *that* away!" The monk insisted, "I have told you that there is nothing left in me. What should I cast away?" Joshu then said, "In that case, keep on carrying it," and he put an end to the question. This monk blew his own trumpet declaring that he had cast away everything, but he was not aware how ignoble it was to make a boast of having cast away every-thing. He was sticking to Oneness, and there-fore not free at all.

There is another famous painting by Haku-in—a portrait of Bodhidharma drawn in a symbolic, free style. On this painting he wrote, "So happy to see you, I have nothing to say!" In the history of Zen as originating in India and transmitted to China and Japan, Bodhidharma is the 28th Patriarch. But in the Chinese develop-ment of Zen history he is considered the First Patriarch of Zen, and is a very important figure. Here, however, in Hakuin's painting, he is not just an historical personage. He symbolizes the essence of Zen, Zen Enlightenment, or the fact of religious experience itself. If we read Hakuin's lines on this painting literally, they comprise nothing but an affectionate, witty remark, "I am glad to see you, after such a long time, and in sheer happiness I can find no words to express myself." The true meaning of these lines, how-ever, is not found in such an interpretation.

After years of hard, assiduous searching, if one finally finds his true spiritual home, would he have any appropriate words to express this new vista? Zen Master Mumon spent six years of hard training with the famous *koan Mu* (nothing-ness). One day when he heard the beating of the drum announcing mealtime, all of a sudden,

77

he attained to Enlightenment. Describing this exquisite moment of Enlightenment after so many years of hard training, he said, "It is like a dumb person trying to explain the dream he had." It is natural that when one comes to this realization opening his eye to a new world of quite a different order, he is unable to find words to express his actual experience.

So far, I have stated some of Hakuin's unique and extraordinary religious activities. With his unusual endowments and ability he was active in writing, preaching and guiding his disciples in *sesshin*. He was the Master who repeatedly stressed the importance of Enlightenment experience which is the very essence and life of Zen. In this way Zen was revived by the advent of this great Zen Master. He gave new life to Zen at a critical time when its spirit was threatening to die out. Thus he is rightly called "The patriarch who revived Zen."

On the Title

Zazen in Japanese consists of two characters, *za* (坐) and *zen* (禅). If we analyze the literal meanings of them, *za* means to sit crosslegged, *zen*, to calmly concentrate one's mind. The Japanese word *zazen* can be traced back to the Sanskrit word *dhyana*. While the Japanese word *zazen* and the Sanskrit *dhyana* are related historically, their real meanings are different in some respects. Today in Japan, the word *zazen* is sometimes used in the sense of quiet sitting thus referring to a form of sitting. In other cases *zazen* is understood as mental concentration by means of quiet sitting. In the latter case the spiritual function of concentration is stressed rather than the form of sitting. In both cases, however, the word is used in the sense similar to *dhyana* and implies discipline and training. In such instances, *zazen* is understood as a means to the attainment of *satori*, Enlightenment.

There are again cases where the same word *zazen* is used in quite a different sense. For instance, Dogen (1200–1253), the founder of Soto Zen in Japan, said, "*Zazen* is not a means of training. It is the Dharma practice of emancipation." And also, "What is essential is *zazen*. Descendants of Buddha should Practice it accordingly. This is the true teaching rightly transmitted." Here *zazen* is used in quite another fashion. *Zazen* in such instances goes beyond the traditional concept of *dhyana*, and it points to "what is essential," and "the true teaching rightly transmitted." It refers to the Zen experience itself in which all of its teachings are included. Here the concept of *zazen* goes be-

yond that of the Sanskrit term *dhyana*. It has
a depth and breadth of quite a different type.

Hui-neng, the Sixth Patriarch (638–713), is
one of those who established Zen in China. He
defined *zazen* as follows: "In the midst of all
good-and-evil, not a thought is aroused in the
mind—this is called *za*. Seeing into one's Self-
nature, not being moved at all—this is called *zen*."
So far as this definition is concerned, *za* does not
mean just to sit cross-legged. It means not to
give rise to discriminating consciousness "in the
midst of all good-and-evil." The ethical expression of good-and-evil is here used to represent
all of our dualistic discriminations to which we
are so liable in our daily life. *Za* is to cast these
all away. It is not just to physically assume a
static sitting posture. *Zen* is, according to Hui-
neng, "seeing into one's Self-nature, and not being
moved at all." In other words, *zen* is to awaken
to our fundamental Self-nature, and not to be
disturbed by the superficial waverings of our
minds. It is nothing else but Enlightenment experience itself. When "a thought is not aroused
in the midst of all good-and-evil," "one's seeing
into his Self-nature" can be realized. Thus in
fact both *za* and *zen* point to the fact of deep
religious experience. The Six Patriarch's definition of *zazen* is therefore the same as that of
Dogen's.

Hakuin's Song of Zazen is a verse representing Zen itself, inclusive and fundamental, and not a song to teach *dhyana*. We have to keep this point in mind when we read the text. *Zazen Wasan* is therefore not a teaching to propagate quiet sitting literally taken, nor is it appropriate to apply the Sanskrit term *dhyana* for *zazen*, for Hakuin's *Zazen Wasan* is the song of "Zen."

I wish to repeat here what I stated at the beginning. Zen is to be understood independent of the Zen School of Buddhism. Zen does not belong inclusively and exclusively to the Zen School of Buddhism. I believe Zen is the universal truth that brings true wisdom and peace to the lives of the people in the world. Any religion or culture should avail itself of whatever spiritual value Zen can offer.

Zen Masters in olden days were also concerned with this point. Dogen, the founder of Soto Zen in Japan, declared, "Anybody who would regard Zen as a school or sect of Buddhism, and call it *Zen-shu*, Zen School, is a devil." In this strong expression he warns us not to make this mistake, and he clarifies the absolute and universal nature of Zen. What Hakuin is pointing out is most definitely Zen, and not the Zen School.

To return to the words in the title, *san* (讚) of *wasan* means a song in praise. A character *wa* (和), which means Japanese is added to it.

In translating *wasan* into English, however, it may not be necessary to include it. This insignificant looking character *wa*, however, reveals the fact that Hakuin had deep affection for the common people. Japan in those days was a country of strict feudal system, and it was the custom of the upper, intellectual class to revere the Chinese language. Serious writings were in Chinese as a rule, just as in Europe, centuries ago, religious and scholastic works were generally written in Latin. Still, Hakuin did not hesitate to break the custom, and he wrote this Song in everyday colloquial Japanese. In our democratic world today, this may not seem important, but in Hakuin's day the situation was different. It revealed his firm determination to propagate the teaching of Zen to everyone without discrimination, and thus reflected his great love for his fellow beings.

On the Structure of the Song

The Song of Zazen can be understood to be an outline of Zen. I will first refer to its "structure." It is not possible to ascertain whether the author Hakuin himself had this structure in mind when he wrote the Song. However, I myself see a systematic structure in the

Song, and believe that interpretation of this kind will help us understand the Song more clearly.

The Song of Zazen consists of forty-four lines, which can be divided into three parts. The first part is a sort of introduction. It comprises of lines 1—14. Here the fundamental principle of Zen teaching is explained; its characteristics and aim clarified. The second part, lines 15—40, corresponds to the body of the text. First Hakuin tells us how great the Mahayana Zen teaching is. Then he emphasizes the fact of Zen experience, and describes the new vista opened by this experience. The third part can be regarded as the conclusion, lines 41—44. Here Hakuin concludes that what Zen aims at is, after all, the completion of Zen personality with which one lives and works in this actual world of ours.

The essential point in each of the above three parts can be summarized by the following three lines repectively:

Part I, Introduction:
"All beings are primarily Buddhas." (1)
—Zen is based on one's original Buddha Nature.

Part II, Main Text:
"And testify to the truth of Self-nature."(30)

83

—One is to attain Enlightenment by going through actual training.

Part III, Conclusion:
"Your person, the body of Buddha."(44)
—Then he lives the Zen life of non-doing.

Thus the first, thirtieth and the last lines are the three main poles of *Zazen Wasan*. The remaining forty-one lines of the verse are explanatory to these. And it is significant that the thirtieth line, "And testify to the truth of Self-nature," which is the core of the whole verse, ties up the first line with the last concluding line.

"All beings are primarily Buddhas" concludes still the abstract truth. It has to be testified in "your person;" it has to be realized by "you" as the "fact." When this "person" accomplishes his Zen personality, he lives as a "true" man, where "to work is Zen, to sit is Zen." The real spirit of Zen exists in this *samadhi* where he actually lives and works out the Truth with his whole life. Thus *Zazen Wasan* can be freely developed to form forty-four lines, or else it can all be reduced into the last one line.

THE SONG OF ZAZEN

Part I: Introduction

"All beings are primarily Buddhas." (1)

At the very beginning of *Zazen Wasan*, Haku-in boldly declares what the principle of Zen doctrine is.   It is vital to fully understand this first line in reading the Song of Zazen. It will further help readers understand Zen teaching.

The Song starts with the words "all beings." The Japanese word for it is *shujo* (衆生), and this is the translation of the Sanskrit term *sattva*. This term *sattva* means "creatures living in the world of ignorance." In a broad sense it includes all living things.   Here, however, we can take it in a less broad sense and interpret it as we human beings.

Next comes the word *Buddhas*, which is not very easy to comprehend. This of course is taken from the Sanskrit *Buddha*. However, this term Buddha, in Japanese *hotoke* (仏), as used today in Japan is quite different from that of its Sanskrit original. The Japanese word *hotoke*, Buddha, is used in the sense of "an holy and absolute being, with supernatural power, who belongs to a totally different sphere. He can often be the Omnicompetent one who controls the destiny of everything in the world." This concept of Buddha is similar to the term God in Christianity. Needless to say there are many differences between them if these two words are precisely studied. What is signified by *Buddha* in Sanskrit however is totally different. It means an enlightened one. According to this interpretation, Buddha is just an enlightened man, or an awakened man in contrast to man in ignorance. In any case he is admired as one who belongs to the same world as we do. This is the basic point in the concept of "Buddha."

What, then, is he enlightened about? What is he awakened to? Subjectively explained, he is awakened to Buddha Nature, or Dharma Nature, which he was primarily born with. Objectively explained, he has realized the eternal truth or the fundamental source of existence. We also call such a person, the one who is awakened to his True Self. In any case, although there is a great difference between an enlightened man and a man in ignorance, Buddha is not an absolute being who exists apart from us and cannot be identified with us. Buddha is therefore a common being, and it can take the plural form. He does not exist apart from historical beings who actually live in this world.

In a Zen text we have the following story. It was in the days of Sakyamuni Buddha. There was a man named Kogaku. He made his livelihood by slaughtering, and he used to kill over one thousand sheep a day. One day, however, this man Kogaku appeared before Sakyamuni. Throwing away his big knife which he used for slaughtering, he declared, "I am one of thousands of Buddhas!" Sakyamuni calmly looked at him for a while, and approved it, saying, "Yes, you are!"

Many important questions are involved in this story, but I will now only refer to the meaning of the term Buddha as used here. According to the Indian thinking of those days, which was bound by the caste system, Kogaku was born with a cursed *karma*, doomed to an ill fate. A butcher was a forsaken man who could not hope for salvation. Yet a butcher with this fate was recognized by Buddha as one of thousands of Buddhas, as one of many enlightened beings.

This interpretation of the term Buddha was taken over by the Chinese Zen Masters of the Tang and Sung dynasties. Zen Masters in the Tang and Sung dynasties left many *mondo* on the question "What is Buddha?" They all took up the question, interpreting Buddha as an enlightened one, and they promoted Zen studies on

87

this basis. I will give you some of the famous *mondo*.

A monk asked Zen Master Sai of Ungo, "What is Buddha?" In reply, the Master said, "Who are you?" Ungo's rebuking reply meant, "You, who have just asked me what Buddha is, are Buddha yourself, aren't you?" Ungo saw Buddha in his actual self.

A monk by the name E-cho asked Hogen Buneki, a Master, "What is Buddha?" "You are E-cho," the Master replied. This reply of Hogen means, "Why do you seek for Buddha apart from E-cho who is sitting here right now? Where E-cho is E-cho through and through, there you see Buddha."

A monk asked Shuzan Shonen, "What is Buddha?" "The bride is riding on a donkey, and the bridegroom is leading it," was Shuzan's reply. This answer describes a couple just married. The bride dressed in her very best is riding on a donkey. The solemn looking bridegroom leads the donkey with the reins in his hand, to take his bride back home. The bride in her wedding costume, and the bridegroom who leads the donkey—aren't they both Buddhas? If I transfer this picture of a newly wedded couple to our modern scene, the bridegroom is driving the car, the bride is sitting next to him. Aren't they both Buddhas as they are? Shuzan says that in his eyes the driver and his companion are both Buddhas.

In Zen texts there are of course an almost innumerable number of answers to this question, "What is Buddha?" They cannot all be classified under the same category. Different answers were given from various angles. Yet it is true that all the answers are based on the idea of Buddha as meaning an enlightened one. In the case of Hakuin's Song of Zazen, Buddha also definitely means an enlightened one. It does not refer to an absolute being or an Omnipotent one who exists apart from us, as the term is commonly understood.

If we read the first part based on this understanding, we see that it declares that we human beings are all enlightened ones. This is a rather surprising assertion. However, an adverb "primarily" is added to the sentence as a condition. We have to realize that the first line is not an unconditional assertion. The proposition that we are primarily Buddhas means that we are all born with the seed, or the potentiality, of being enlightened ones. Although we were born with such potentiality, for the moment it has not yet been awakened or developed. In any event, the final aim of Zen is to make an ideal Zen personality. It teaches us to find the way to it in our own selves as we actually live here and now, and not in something outside ourselves. This should be the great message for human beings, that we have this potentiality in ourselves.

There is a Zen phrase, "The brilliant gem is in your hand." It is interesting that in Japan we often come across a hanging scroll with this phrase in tea ceremony rooms. Literally, this phrase means that the brilliant gem which everybody values so much and eagerly seeks for is in the hand of he who is seeking for it. Or, we can say that the true and invaluable jewel is not like diamonds and pearls that can be found elsewhere outside. You are born with it, and it is in your own hand. The brilliant gem here symbolizes Buddha Nature, or Dharma Nature. This Zen phrase is a metaphor to teach that all beings are primarily Buddhas. What Zen tries to do is to awaken our innate Buddha Nature and to allow us to live as enlightened ones based on this realization. This is the aim of Zen.

The question we have to clarify next would be "What is this Buddha Nature, or Dharma Nature, with which we are born?" I will give you a simile which has been used from olden days. In Buddhism, the wisdom of an enlightened one is often called the wisdom of a big round mirror. The circle is a symbol of this big perfect mirror. The mirror is thoroughly egoless and mindless. If a flower comes, it reflects a flower;

if a bird comes, it reflects a bird. It shows a beautiful object as beautiful, an ugly object as ugly. Everything is revealed as it is. There is no discriminating mind or self-consciousness on the part of the mirror. If something comes, the mirror just reflects it; if it disappears, the mirror just lets it disappear. Whether it likes or not, no traces of anything are left behind. Such non-attachment, the state of no-mind, or the truly free working of a mirror is compared here to the pure and lucid wisdom of Buddha.

Further, everyone is treated equally in front of a mirror. It does not discriminate between the rich and the poor. It does not make the rich and the distinguished look beautiful because they are special; nor does it make the poor particularly ugly. Male and female, old men and children, all are treated equally in front of the mirror. For the mirror, a big mountain and a tiny small stone are equal. A diamond and a piece of glass are equal. Everything is equal. Such an immaculate and lucid mind, thoroughly fair and impartial with no discrimination at all, is called Buddha Nature, Dharma Nature or Self-nature. Zen teaches that we human beings primarily have this Buddha Nature or Dharma Nature in ourselves. The one who is awakened to this truth is called an enlightened one, a Buddha. A mirror is a good simile, but it lacks this function of awakening. This is the difference between human beings and mirrors.

We, however, in our actual life, cannot easily accept such a teaching. We tend to think that Buddhas and human beings are totally different, and regard Buddha as existing outside ourselves, high and above. Hakuin tries to correct this misunderstanding. He refers to the relation of water and ice to illustrate this mistake.

"Like water and ice, (2)
  There is no ice apart from water; (3)
  There are no Buddhas apart from beings." (4)

As you know, water can be warm, but ice is cold. Water has no shape but ice has shape. Water is liquid and is free to flow anywhere, but ice is solid and unmoving. Water helps plants to grow and gives life to fish, but ice damages plants and kills fish. Like this, ice and water are just opposite. They appear essentially different in nature. The ingredients of ice and water, however, are exactly the same. If we heat ice a little, it immediately turns to water. Ice is just a temporary form of water; when water loses its temperature, it assumes this temporary appearance. Therefore, if we realize that ice is water, the truth that we human beings are Buddhas and cannot be otherwise will be understood.

Here I must invite your attention to the following important point. To understand the truth is one thing; to prove the truth in one's own actual living is quite another thing. They should not be confused. Ice has to be heated to become water. It means that one has to go through actual training to testify to the truth in his own person. If he just remains knowing the truth, and never testifies to it, he cannot be an enlightened one.

"Not knowing how close the Truth is to them, (5)
 Beings seek for it afar—what a pity! (6)
 It is like those who being in water (7)
 Cry out for water, feeling thirst." (8)

We human beings are in the closest relationship with Buddha, the enlightened one. Not knowing it, we turn our eyes outward and try to seek. How foolish, what a pity, Hakuin regretfully comments. If it is really like the relationship between ice and water, then we are Buddhas *as we are.* So he goes on to say, "It is like those who being in water, Cry out for water, feeling thirst."

Years ago, a Japanese steamship for the first time went up the great Amazon river in South America. It was a long voyage, and they ran out of drinking water. Fortunately a British ship came by. The Japanese ship asked them by signal, "Have you drinking water to spare?" They signaled back, "Put your buckets down into the water, if you please." The surprised Japanese crew did as instructed, and sure enough it was drinking water. For the Japanese crew who were used to seeing small rivers in Japan, the River Amazon was too big for them to recognize as a river. They thought they were still in the ocean. Aren't we, without realizing it, making such mistakes everyday?

In a Zen text there is such a *mondo*. An of Chokei asked Master Hyakujo: "Students want to understand Buddha. What is Buddha?" Hyakujo answered, "It is like a man who seeks for an ox while riding on it." Chokei went on to ask: "What happens if he realizes it?" "It is like a man who returns home riding on the ox." In this *mondo*, Hyakujo is also pointing out the foolishness of crying out for water while being in the midst of it.

Hakuin tells us another story in order to clarify the relationship between ordinary beings and enlightened ones.

"It is like the rich man's son, (9)
Who has lost his way among the poor." (10)

This refers to the famous parable of "A Rich Man and his Missing Son," which is found in a

Buddhist sutra called *Hoke-kyo* (*Saddharma-pundarika-sutra*), and these two lines are taken from it. I will briefly tell this story in outline.

There lived in India an extremely rich nobleman with only one son, but one day he was either kidnapped or lost. The father did all he could to find his beloved son, all in vain. Years passed without his discovering his whereabouts, and as the father got older, his yearning for his missing son increased the more. One day as the rich man was looking out of his upstairs window, a young beggar came to his house, was given something and was about to leave the gate. The rich man saw the face of the beggar and jumped up in surprise, for he recognized his missing son. At once he called his servants and said, "Bring that young beggar here." Several servants ran after the beggar and tried to bring him back. The young man refused to return saying, "Forgive me, please. I shall never come to your house again. Although I am a beggar, I haven't done anything wrong." "No, no, we aren't scolding you. Our master just wishes to see you," the servants assured him, but they could not induce him to return. On the contrary, he got more afraid and began to tremble, saying, "I have nothing to do with such a great nobleman." Finally the servants had to return and report their failure to the master.

The rich man, full of affection for his son, gave an order to one of his young servants to disguise himself as a beggar like his son and to befriend him. When this servant-beggar thought the time right, he said to the young beggar, the rich man's son, "I have found a good job. The work is not too hard, and the wages are good. They will also provide us with a small room. Why don't you come and try it with me?" Thus both of them were employed as gardeners to the rich man.

The young man worked as a gardener for a while. When he became accustomed to this situation, the rich man promoted him to being a house servant. When he did well in all his work, the rich man then put him in charge of his property. Eventually the son was appointed his secretary to stay close to him and take care of all his responsibilities.

Years passed. The rich man grew older. Realizing he would not live much longer he gathered his relatives and friends, and introduced the young man saying, "This youth is in fact my own son, who disappeared when he was a little child," and handed over all his property and status to his son.

Sakyamuni Buddha attained to Enlightenment when he saw the morning star twinkling in the sky at dawn, after six years of the hardest searching. It is recorded that Sakyamuni cried out, with exceeding joy, "How wonderful, how wonderful! Everybody is endowed with the wisdom and appearance of Tathagata!" This exclamation of Sakyamuni is the same as saying "All beings are primarily Buddhas!" The people who heard Sakyamuni say this, fled from him. The populace did not even listen to him, saying instead, "How absurd! We are so sinful, greedy and ill-tempered. How could we be enlightened beings? Don't deceive us."

Sakyamuni therefore had to adopt the method of "teaching Dharma in accordance with the capability of each." First he had to preach, "You are sinful creatures and are in defilement. Repent, and purify yourselves. Do good for your future happiness. Observe the precepts." Then he went on to say, "You all think that there is you, yourselves, and there is the world; there is ignorance and there is enlightenment. However, everything with form changes. Everything in the world is just a result of causes and conditions. The happiness of life is to come to this realization and live with no attachment." The populace now came gladly to listen to him. In this way, Sakyamuni gradually went on to expound higher teachings, and finally declared the great truth saying, "The time has come for me to show you the Truth. Everyone listen to me carefully. All

Buddhas appear in this world in order to awaken human beings to the true wisdom." At this final declaration, the populace could for the first time accept the great truth.

By means of metaphors and parables Hakuin tries to clarify Zen teaching and the general human situation which he likens to crying out for water thirsting, though being in the midst of water.

"The reason why beings transmigrate through
　　　the six worlds (11)
　Is because they are lost in the darkness of
　　　ignorance. (12)
　Wandering from darkness to darkness, (13)
　How can they ever be free from
　　　birth-and-death?" (14)

It is because we are not awakened to the truth that we have to wander from darkness to darkness and are unable to leave the world of ignorance. He thus again emphasizes the truth that all beings are primarily Buddhas, and reminds us that it is only because we are blind to this truth that we cannot be enlightened ones.

"The reason why beings transmigrate through the six worlds" reflects a simple view of life and death entertained by the Indian people in olden days. I understand that there are still many in

India who believe in this reincarnation even today. They believed that when human beings
pass away, their souls do not die, but forever
keep on transmigrating, according to the merit
of their good or bad deeds while alive, through
the six worlds. Their next destinations would
be pre-determined. The six worlds are: 1) hell
full of all sorts of trials and sufferings; 2) the
world of beasts of various shapes; 3) the world
of starvation; 4) the fighting world where bloody
struggles are going on day and night; 5) this
human world of ours; and 6) the celestial world,
full of joy. A man, after his death, would have
to be reborn in one of these six worlds depending on the *karma* accumulated while he was alive.

The "reason" here means the causes and conditions in the law of causality. There are direct
and indirect causes for an effect, but conditions
are needed to bring about the effect. Conditions
are powers to help causes develop their effect,
but in many cases conditions have much greater
influences on the outcome than the causes. For
human beings who live in the law of causality,
both causes and conditions are vitally important.
Thus we keep on transmigrating through the six
worlds in the most intricate meshes of causes and
conditions. The decisive "reason" for reincarnation, however, Hakuin says, is our ignorance
to the Truth. In other words, our blind instinct

which is unawakened to the Truth. If this blind instinct could be awakened to the Truth, we should be able to cut off our transmigration and our emancipation would then be accomplished; we would be enlightened ones.

In line 14, Hakuin speaks of being free from birth-and-death. This is the same as cutting off the transmigration of ignorance. Zen plainly and clearly tells us to cut off the transmigration of ignorance by awakening to the Buddha mind with which we were born. In other words, we are to effect this fundamental inner conversion of our personality and directly realize that "All beings are primarily Buddhas."

Part II: Main Text of *Zazen Wasan*

The second part of Hakuin's Song of Zazen, that is, lines 15—40, corresponds to the body of the text. The Second Part is however rather long and complicated in substance. As it is difficult to explain each detail, I will lay emphasis on several important lines, and just briefly explain the other lines.

"As to Zazen taught in the Mahayana, (15)
    No amount of praise can exhaust its merits." (16)

The phrase "Zazen taught in the Mahayana" sounds technical and formal, but it can be understood as a phrase referring to Zen itself, fundamental and inclusive. Zen, or Zazen is the essence of Mahayana Buddhism.

I referred to this to some extent in my explanation of the title "*Zazen Wasan.*" In lines 15 and 16, Hakuin states that Zazen taught in the Mahayana, that is, Zen, is worthy of every possible praise and admiration. He then goes on to say why.

"The Six Paramitas, beginning with the
    Giving, (17)

101

Observing the Precepts and other good deeds,
variously enumerated, (18)
As Nembutsu, Repentance, and so on— (19)
All are finally reducible to Zazen." (20)

Here he clarifies how Zen is different from
other Buddhist teachings in general. The Sanskrit
term *Paramita* means "to attain to the other
shore of Enlightenment." It is, in other words,
a means to attain Enlightenment. Buddhism
generally teaches people to faithfully practice the
six virtues, i.e. 1) *dana* (giving), 2) *sila* (observing the precepts), 3) *virya* (spirit of manhood),
4) *ksanti* (humility), 5) *dhyana* (meditation),
and 6) *prajna* (true wisdom). In the text only
the first two, giving and observing the precepts,
are mentioned, and the rest are omitted.

Hakuin further refers to various training
methods such as Nembutsu (recitation of
Buddha's name), repentance, etc., but maintains
that fundamentally speaking, all these religious
practices are finally covered by Zen and return to
it. He thus illustrates the basic and transcendental nature of Zen.

"The merit of even a single sitting in Zazen. (21)
Erases the countless sins accumulated
in the past. (22)
Where then are there the evil paths

to misguide us? (23)
The Pure Land cannot be far away." (24)

Of course different interpretations based on the primary viewpoint of Zen can be given to these lines. Here, however, we may take them as praise of Mahayana Zen. There is a saying in Zen, "If one sits for ten minutes, he is ten-minute Buddha."

"Those who, even once, in all humility, (25)
Listen to this Truth, (26)
Praise it and faithfully follow it, (27)
Will be endowed with innumerable merits." (28)

Even should a person, for some reason, not be able to devote himself to actual Zazen practice, but hear this teaching of Mahayana Zen, believe it to be true and completely entrust himself to it with joy, he will certainly be exceedingly blessed. Here Hakuin is again praising Mahayana Zen. In these twelve lines, from 17 to 28, Hakuin explains how Zen is different from other Buddhist practices. He reveals his critical opinion of them, and illustrates how praiseworthy Zen is.

The most important part of the Song of Zazen, however, is in the next four lines, 29 through 32. This is the core of Zen teaching, and Zen is based upon, and developed from these four lines:

"But if you turn your eyes within yourselves (29)
  And testify to the truth of Self-nature— (30)
  The Self-nature that is no-nature, (31)
  You will have gone beyond the ken of
      sophistry." (32)

The first two lines in particular "But if you
turn your eyes within yourselves"/"And testify
to the truth of Self-nature," are of the utmost
importance. The spirit and life of Zen exist here.
First I will take up the phrase "To turn your
eyes within yourselves." An old Zen Master
said, commenting on this, "One should not be
diverted to all the surrounding objectivity, but
should turn directly to his own Nature. This is
'Turning to and Reflecting on Oneself.'" The
Truth is to be sought inwardly, within oneself.
One should not turn one's eye outwardly seeking
for the Truth in the relativistic outside world.
This is the basic characteristic of Zen that it
always seeks for the fundamental Truth within
oneself, and never in anything outside. Why
are we to seek for the Truth inwardly within ourselves? That is because "All beings are primarily
Buddhas," as Hakuin declares at the beginning
of the Song. The whole teaching of Zen is based
on the realization of this Truth. In this aspect,
Zen shows the way to the fundamental solution
of the self.

The word Self-nature, used here, means one's basic nature which he primarily has, deep at the bottom of his personality. It is the True Self, in contrast to the superficial self. It is the "Primary Buddha Nature," referred to by Hakuin at the beginning of the Song, when he says "All beings are primarily Buddhas." "To testify to the truth of Self-nature" is to awaken to our primary Buddha Nature which we have deep in ourselves, and to become enlightened beings ourselves.

Our attention is called here to the word "testify." Hakuin does not talk about "knowing Self-nature," or "understanding Self-nature." Instead of such intellectual expressions, he uses the experiential word "testify." "To testify" is to experience it with one's whole being as actual fact. One's whole personality accepts the truth of Self-nature as the living truth. It may not be difficult to *talk about* this experience of awakening to "Self-nature" or "True Self" which we have deep at the bottom of our personalities, but to come to this realization experientially as the fact of one's own actual experience, is not easy at all. It is so very difficult that it cannot be easily attained by ordinary people. Why is it so difficult? Because, although we may have True Nature deep within ourselves, in actuality we are covered by the many thick veiled layers of dualistically discriminating consciousness.

In the Song, Hakuin simply says, "And testify to the truth of Self-nature." In order to actually testify to it, however, we have to first of all abolish all of our ordinary and superficial dualistic consciousness. This hard, painful and almost desperate inner struggle to smash ordinary dualistic consciousness is called "training in Zen" or "Zen discipline." After long and trying inner struggle, when one has smashed the superficial self, one is for the first time awakened to his True Self, and has realization as an enlightened one. Shido Bunan, a Japanese Zen Master in in the mid-Tokugawa period, has the following famous Zen verse:

"Die while alive, and be completely dead,
    Then do whatever you will, all is good."

Shido Bunan uses grandiose words as "Die while alive, and be completely dead." But this is the inevitable process one must go through in the course of Zen training. If I explain this verse in simpler language, it is "to smash up ordinary dualistic consciousness." When one really goes through this inner experience and is resurrecting in the world of consciousness, a new vista opens up unto him. He attains true freedom and peace. Shido Bunan says, describing it, "Do whatever you will, all is good."

If we look back at the past history of Zen, there are many examples of Zen Masters who have gone through hard and trying disciplines. The individual's training may differ from person to person, depending upon talent, surroundings, living circumstances, etc., but I can still declare that there is not a single case where one is enlightened without going through the hard and difficult training process. Let me give you an example—the record of how a famous Zen Master testified to the truth of Self-nature.

Kyogen was a Master active in the ninth century in China. After his ordination as a monk, he followed first the general course of a Buddhist monk, devoting himself to the scholastic studies of Zen. He was intrinsically brilliant and diligent. Soon he was reputed to be a learned Buddhist scholar. Kyogen however came to realize that scholastic studies alone would not fully satisfy him. Finally he decided to study Zen, and he became a disciple of Master Isan. Isan wished somehow to make Kyogen realize how utterly incapable his intellectual learning was in answering the fundamental questions. With the hope of inducing Kyogen to plunge into the abyss of the Great Doubt, Isan asked him: "I am interested neither in the scholastic knowledge you have accumulated so far, nor in whatever teachings you might find in sutras. Just give me a word of yours on your Self before you were born, when the distinction of east and west did not exist." Kyogen was naturally at a loss as to how to answer such a question. With all the intellectual ability he could muster he tried to somehow give satisfactory answers to it, and he brought them to Isan. Isan however rejected every one of them saying, "It is what is written in a book, and not your own." Kyogen felt like facing an imperious iron wall, and did not know what to do.

Our knowledge and scholarship are of course very convenient for us in getting along in the world, and they are very important, too. But they cannot bring about the evolution of personality. They fail to touch the fundamental basis of personality. Knowledge and intellect in this regard yield to the deepness of experience. We may know that water can satisfy thirst. This knowledge, however, has its real significance when one actually has the experience of having his thirst satisfied by drinking water. Without the experience, he may remain just a pedant.

Kyogen was driven to despair, and he finally came to the Master and implored him: "Have compassion on me, and please teach me." But no matter how earnestly he pleaded with the Master, the Master flatly refused to clarify further, saying, "Even if I show you the answer, it is *my* answer. It has nothing to do with *your* understanding which should be experienced and obtained by yourself."

Kyogen now shut himself up in a room and went over every possible book and record. He could not however find any solution which he could present to Isan as his answer. In an abyss of despair, he tore up all the notes and records of his past, studies saying, "Painted cake cannot satisfy hunger." He dispiritedly left Isan, deploring his ill-fate, and became a grave keeper to the Zen Master E-chu living in a small secluded retreat. Though his biography does not give us any details in regard to Kyogen's state of mind after he left Isan, he most probably was in sheer despair and continued searching within himself for "the Absolute," which was like facing an impregnable fortress. His inner Zen consciousness was getting more intensified and was waiting for the opportunity to break out.

One day he was cleaning the garden. He carried rubbish and trash in a basket and threw them away in the bamboo grove behind his house. A small stone in the trash hit the bamboo with a rap. At this, he felt he himself and the whole universe were all smashed up, and his inner darkness was at once dispersed. He broke into laughter. This was the moment when he finally attained to Great Enlightenment. He "testified to the truth of his 'True Self even before he was born'." Kyogen changed his clothes, burnt incense, and worshipped in the direction where his teacher Isan lived. He thanked Isan saying, "The compassion of my teacher is greater than that of even my parents. Had he explained to me and showed me the answer, I should never have been able to have this great joy!" Kyogen's story is written in a Zen text.

Thus, "to testify" is "to prove 'it' as an actual experience of one's own person." "To testify" is fundamentally different from "to know." "To testify" is possible when one breaks through his discriminating consciousness, and plunges into a new world. This experience opens up for him a new vista on human life. He has been reborn as a totally different personality.

I will give you another story from the biography of the Zen Master Hogen (d. 958), who lived in the ninth century China, to show how one came "to testify to the truth of Self-nature."

A monk came to Hogen's monastery. Some days passed, but this monk did not come to see the Master at all. One day Hogen called him up and said, "You have never come to see me on the subject of Zen studies. Why?" The monk replied, "I have already obtained *satori*. Therefore I have no need to ask you anything more." Hogen said: "Well, then tell me what kind of *satori* you have obtained." The monk proudly stated: "While I was staying at another monastery before coming here, one day I asked the Master, 'What is Buddha?' He replied: '*Hei-tei-doji Rai-gu-ka!*' At this answer I at once realized that it was so. This is my *satori*."

"*Hei-tei-doji*" is the deity of fire. "*Rai-gu-ka*" means "to seek after fire." "*Hei-tei-doji Rai-gu-ka*" therefore is the same as saying that Buddha is seeking after Buddha. Primarily all beings are Buddhas, therefore there is no need for us to wander around seeking for a Buddha. "I have been a Buddha myself. Everything is good as it is. I realized the foolishness of further seeking after Buddha." This was what the monk meant by his reply.

Hearing it, Hogen flatly disapproved and said: "It just shows that your *satori* is a fake." At this unexpected severe reproof, the monk was much offended and he walked out of Hogen's monastery saying, "Why should I keep on staying with such an unreasonable old man?" He thus left the monastery angrily, but while walking for several miles, he began to feel somehow uneasy, and this uneasiness gradually increased in his mind. He stopped walking and reflected, "It is not likely that a great Master like Hogen would abuse me so severely without any reason. I might have been in the wrong to so easily get angry." The monk thus decided to return to Hogen. He came again to Hogen and asked him to kindly teach him.

At this Hogen said, "I am glad that you have realized that you were in the wrong, and have thus come back to study again. If you had gone without realizing it, it would have ruined your life!" Then the Master told him, "Ask me the question again!" So the monk asked the Master anew: "What is Buddha?" At this Hogen lifted up his voice and said. "*Hei-tei-doji Rai-gu-ka!*" He gave exactly the same answer as the monk had previously presented. Strange to say, however, this same question, and the same answer enabled the monk to attain to the true *satori* this time. The monk, forgetting himself, prostrated himself in front of the Master, and thanked him for his compassionate teaching.

This famous *mondo* presents many important questions for us to consider. I should like to reflect on the following points in particular. The monk asked his first teacher when he was studying under him, "What is Buddha?" The Master answered and said: "*Hei-tei-doji Rai-gu-ka!*" (The deity of fire is seeking after fire.) The monk said that at this he came to realize that it was as if "Buddha is seeking for Buddha," and "Beings are therefore Buddhas themselves." This, however, in fact remained his intellectual understanding only. It did not reach the depths of his personality to effect the fundamental change. In other words, his so-called realization did not yet "testify to the truth of Self-nature." The clear and piercing eye of Hogen saw this and the monk once more had to seek after True Enlightenment. This next time he was able to break through all of his intellectual understanding and he experienced "testifying to the truth of Self-nature." It was because of the monk's genuine religious aspiration and his earnest and sincere searching that he finally could have this exquisite moment of joy.

This *mondo* suggests another important question in regard to actual Zen training. There are two tendencies, or approaches, in studying Zen: One is psychological and the other is philsophical. Ideally speaking, these two aspects of Zen should of course be interfused and unified in one personality. Actually, however, it is not easy to carry on Zen training in this ideal way, and one tends to be inclined in one direction or the other.

The monk told Hogen that, at the words of his first teacher that "The deity of fire is seeking after fire," he came to the realization that it was like "Buddha seeking after Buddha," and that "I am Buddha myself." The story does not give us any more details, but it is possible that this monk's realization had, after all, some truth in it, and we should not perhaps just dismiss it as insignificant. "Fire seeks after fire," can be interpreted as a state of *samadhi* where the subject, the seeker, and the object, what is sought after, are just one. This state of *samadhi*, however, often tends to be just a "psychological state of being one with something," and lacks the basic *prajna* (true wisdom) to develop. Hogen saw that the monk's *satori* still remained in just such a psychological state of *samadhi*, and failed to work out into *prajna*, true wisdom. He therefore stated that his *satori* was not yet a true *satori*. Then the monk, being rebuked, hesitated in his mind, and began to ask "Why?" This doubt engrossed his whole being. His Zen consciousness was intensified by doubt though he was not aware of it. Doubt is related to wisdom. He put the same question again to Hogen, but his inner spiritual condition was totally different on the second occasion. Hogen gave exactly the same reply, and this had the effect of breaking through his Great Doubt, and enabled him to open a new eye of wisdom. He now had the experience of "testifying to the truth of Self-nature," which was deep enough to fundamentally change his personality.

Ancient Zen Masters taught that "Under Great Doubt there is Great Enlightenment." To have Great Doubt is the start, or a necessary condition for carrying on Zen training and its consequence is the break-up of dualistic intellect. Zen has the lucidity of breaking entirely through the dualistic intellect. Zen experience has this philosophical depth in it. Hakuin, the author of this Song of Zazen, had himself gone through most intense discipline. One day at twenty-four years of age, when he was doing *zazen* throughout the night, the bell announced the dawn and the thick clouds which had covered his mind were completely broken through. It is recorded that he jumped with joy. At this mysterious moment his spiritual eye was opened to a totally different new dimension.

These stories indicate that actual Zen training is absolutely necessary. Without it Zen lacks its life and spirit. Zen Masters in the early stages of Zen history were religious geniuses with strong will and endowments. They disciplined themselves and broke through the barrier of dualism by themselves. These Zen Masters wished somehow to share the great joy of Zen experience with others who might not be capable of attaining Enlightenment by themselves, unaided. Because of the compassionate consideration of the ancient Masters, a kind of artificial training method was worked out in the course of history. Hakuin is especially famous in this regard. He established a new training method, and tried to encourage as many people as possible to attain Zen experience. Most of the Zen monasteries in Japan today are following Hakuin's examples.

Personal aptitudes of each individual, however, are reflected to a considerable degree in actual Zen training. That is, some Zen Masters may be more emotionally inclined, while others may be more philosophically-minded. Depending on such individual tendencies, various rather peculiar training methods are adopted by some teachers.

Recently in particular, I have heard that a variety of scientifically prepared "drugs for Enlightenment" such as LSD are becoming popular. By the use of drugs they hope to bring about certain psychological effect similar to Zen experience, without going through the hardships of traditional Zen training. Although I am not qualified to comment on these drugs, as I have never taken any myself, I should like to say this much: It may be true that the effect which such scientifically prepared drugs produce may have some superficial resemblance to some aspects of Zen experience, but it goes no further, and remains no more than that. In other words, they produce a kind of feeling or a psychological state of mind. When the effect of the drug is gone, the psychological experience one may have had is also weakened and dispersed, and does not endure as living fact.

The point here is, Zen experience effects a fundamental change in oneself, philosophical and intellectual, as well as psychological. It is the total conversion of one's personality to where one is reborn with absolute freedom and creativity. I cannot assent, therefore, to the idea of attempting to taste Zen experience by means of drugs. Only hard, difficult searching processes result in creating firm, and sound personalities.

No verbal expression can fully describe the fact of "testifying to the truth of Self-nature." Master Mumon said, "It is like a dumb person who had a dream. He has had it. That's all." One may utter a cry of joy, but words all fail to sufficiently convey the experince. Human beings are however living creatures, and based on their experience, they naturally express themselves in some direction. Their new activities of expressing themselves are, however, no longer restrained by the old established conceptual frames. They now live in the creative world of God, often breaking the rules of common-sense, and develop their own creative expressions.

To this point Hakuin says in lines 31 and 32: "[When you realize] the Self-nature that is no-nature, You will have gone beyond the ken of sophistry." He tells us that logical or verbal efforts are of no use here. No-nature of course

117

does not mean "empty void." It refers to the truth of quite another order, where the dualism of being and non-being are both transcended. It is therefore the realm where logical intellectualizations are of no use.

In lines 33 through 40, Hakuin describes the realm "beyond the ken of sophistry." It is the world 'seen through the eye of an enlightened one, the inner life developed by one who has "testified to the truth of Self-nature."

"The gate of the oneness of cause and effect is opened;" (33)

Cause comes first in time, and then effect follows. Once you cut off the complications of discriminating consciousness and testify to the truth of Self-nature, you transcend the dualism of before-and-after, long-and-short, and are the master of time. Such a person is no longer restricted by time, but creates it and utilizes it as his own. A seed has within itself eternal past and eternal future. It is from this subjectivity that cause and effect are developed. It is nonsensical to make a distinction between cause and effect within the seed.

Once Joshu made a famous statement on time for his monks: "You are being utilized by the twenty-four hours. As for me, I am utilizing

118

the twenty-four hours." He will never be enslaved by time; he is the master of time and makes free use of it. This absolute freedom is possible for those who live in the oneness of cause and effect.

"The path of non-duality and non-trinity
    runs straight ahead." (34)

There is a famous phrase in *Hoke-kyo* (*Saddharmapundarika-sutra*): "There is only the Dharma of One Vehicle; no duality, no trinity." In referring to it Hakuin says that there is only the Dharma of One Vehicle. The Dharma of One Vehicle means the "Only One Truth." In other words there is just one "Mahayana Zen," which teaches us nothing else but to "testify to the truth of Self-nature." This is the fundamental truth to which all of our life should finally return; from which everything in our life should be created.

"Your form being the form of no-form, (35)
    Your going-and-returning takes place nowhere
      but where you are;" (36)

These lines mean, in plainer language, that the one who has testified to the truth of Self-nature would never be attached to or restricted

119

by objects and conditions surrounding him. He can therefore live with absolute freedom. Various interpretations have been given to this contradictory expression "the form of no-form" since olden days. I do not have time here to comment on these, and will just give a familiar illustration.

A man is working hard gardening, dressed in soiled working clothes of a gardener. When he is notified of a visitor, he takes off his working clothes, puts on a clean dress, and goes to greet the guest as a host. Which is his true self, that of a gardener, or of a host? With the form of no-form we live freely anywhere, under any circumstances.

"Your thought being the thought of
    no-thought, (37)
Your singing-and-dancing is none other than
    the voice of Dharma." (38)

"The thought of no-thought" makes a couplet with "the form of no-form." Of course it describes the inner life of the one who has testified to the truth of Self-nature. "The form of no-form" is an external description of it, while "the thought of no-thought" is a psychological expression. Shido Bunan has a famous saying, "No-thought does not mean 'without thought,' but 'no defiled thought'." "No defiled thought" again is same as "True Thought," and it is the state of mind free from the defilement of dualistic discrimination. Various interpretations have been given, too, to the concept of "no-thought" from ancient times, but I am not going to refer to them here.

In Japan "no-thought is often likened to the "infant-like mind." The non-defiled mind of an infant has no traces of discrimination, between good-and-evil, you-and-I, and so it is as lucid as a mirror. It is fair, impartial and is absolutely free.

"How boundless and free is the sky of
    Samadhi! (39)
How refreshingly bright, the moon of the
    Fourfold Wisdom!" (40)

Hakuin compares the spirituality of an enlightened man to the moon shining in the clear sky. In this literary metaphor, he uses some traditional Buddhist terminology.

"*Samadhi*" now generally accepted as a Japanese word, originally was a Sanskrit term meaning, the immaculate state of mind. It is, to put it in another way, dynamic oneness, where subject and object are one. The thought of no-thought sounds very psychological, but *samadhi* is characteristically a dynamic expression.

The world we usually live in is built on dualistic discriminations: subject is discriminated from object, I from you, the seer from the seen, etc. Zen tells us that there is another way of living, of a different dimension. It asks us to open our eyes to the realm where subject and object are not yet separated, and I and you are one; and then to live and work in this new dimension. A Zen Master, poetically describing such Zen life, says:

"If I scoop the water, the moon is in
    my hands;
If I pluck a flower, fragrant is my robe."

If I scoop the water, I myself am the water and reflect the moon. If I pick up a flower, I am the flower myself and the whole of my body emits fragrance. In this way a Zen man lives in the world. No possible discriminations are here to disturb him. He is completely free, vastly limitless. Hakuin says, "How boundless and free is the sky of Samadhi!"

The "Fourfold Wisdom" means four varieties of Enlightenment wisdom. Needless to say, in the true Zen experience there cannot be four kinds of different Enlightenment. What Hakuin tries to do here is to illustrate the characteristics of Zen Enlightenment from four typical working aspects. The Fourfold Wisdom shows the inner spiritual structure of the one who has testified to the truth of Self-nature. The four aspects are named as follows: 1) Wisdom of a Big Round Mirror, 2) Wisdom of Equality, 3) Wisdom of True Perceiving, and 4) Wisdom of True Working.

One should never misunderstand, however, and think that Zen has four different grades or worlds. "To testify to the truth of Self-nature" is to open one's spiritual eye to a new vista—to be born anew with an enlightened personality. Four different explanations are given just to show how this enlightened personality works out under different conditions. Once enlightened, all of the Fourfold Wisdom are naturally accomplished in him. Hakuin compares it to the bright full moon and says, "How refreshingly bright, the moon of the Fourfold Wisdom!"

To summarize the main text and repeat the points: The new vista which has been opened to the one who has testified to the truth of Self-nature is really beyond all description and sophistry, for it is the message of a realm of truly another dimension. Hakuin, trying to somehow communicate it to us, speaks of "the oneness of cause and effect," "the straight path of non-duality and non-trinity," "the form of no-form," "the boundless and free sky of Samadhi," and "the refreshingly bright moon of the Fourfold Wisdom." All the while Hakuin is telling us that Zen is for each of us to "Testify to the truth of Self-nature," to live a new life with significance of another order.

Part III: Conclusion

"At this moment what is there that you lack? (41)
    Nirvana presents itself before you, (42)
    Where you stand is the Land of Purity. (43)
    Your person, the body of Buddha." (44)

As I stated earlier, Hakuin's Song of Zazen can be taken as an outline of Zen. These last four lines, though very short, are its conclusion.

Hakuin says: "At this moment what is there that you lack?" What does he mean by "this moment"? What kind of time could this be? From the context it is apparent that it refers to the moment when one has testified to the truth of Self-nature. We should not, however, just read it literally from the viewpoint of the structure of the Song alone. In this simple phrase "at this moment," True Time which goes beyond ordinary time is pointed out, and we have to have the eye to read it in the phrase. We generally think that so-called time flows on a straight line from eternal past towards eternal future, and we lead our lives on this straight line of time, dividing it up into long and short, before and after. It is obvious, however, as long as we interpret time like this, we are always bound by time, restricted by time, and enslaved by time. If we want to be truly free and know the happiness of independent life, we have to break through such restrictions of time.

Joshu was a famous Zen Master of the Tang dynasty in China. One day a disciple asked Joshu, "What is the Zen which was introduced into China from India by Bodhidharma many years ago? Joshu immediately retorted, "What is the use of talking about such an old story? What is your Zen here at this moment?" For Joshu, true Zen is shining and alive at this very moment at this very place—"here-now." It exists neither in the story of the past, nor in the expectation of the future. More precisely speaking, "here-now" is eternity itself, in which both before and after, long and short are enveloped. I should like to call such time Religious Time, or Zen Time, over against relative time which is measured by tools or some set standard. We should realize then that "at this moment" refers to Religious Time.

I once read an interesting story concerning time. It was in the sixth century in China— about the time Bodhidharma introduced Zen to China from India. In those days, there was a strict Buddhist precept that priests and monks should not eat after twelve o'clock noon, which, monks of the Theravada Buddhist school observe even today. There lived a devout Buddhist emperor called Butei (Emperor Wu). One day, he gathered a number of Buddhist monks and priests for a convention and entertained them to lunch. For some reason, however, when lunch was served it was already past twelve. Emperor Wu said: "Pretty soon it will be twelve noon. Let us have lunch." Naturally the question arose in the congregation whether they should eat because it was already after twelve. One of the priests, however, suggested, "Since the emperor says it is before noon, perhaps it would be in order for us to eat." Everybody agreed to it, and all broke the precept and had lunch.

We have to realize that True Time definitely exists indifferent to the relative time which we temporarily set for our convenience. Hakuin uses the phrase "at this moment" in line 41. "At this moment" refers to Religious Time, which definitely exists beyond relative time provisionally set by man according to human measurement by tools and machines. For a man who lives in such Religious Time, there is nothing he has to seek outside himself; there is nothing he lacks.

How can such a truly free life be developed? Hakuin says, in the next line, it is possible because "Nirvana presents itself before you." *Nirvana* is a Sanskrit term which means extinction. Although Hakuin uses its Chinese translation "*jakumetsu*" (寂滅) here in this Song, the term *Nirvana* is usually accepted as a Buddhist term, and is a Japanese word now. I will not, however, engage in the etymological explanation of the word *Nirvana*. It can be interpreted simply as the fact of "testifying to the truth of Self-nature," or the *satori* experience of Zen. "Nirvana presents itself before you." therefore, means that *satori*—Enlightenment—presents itself before you." If line 41 is referring to Religious Time, "Nirvana presents itself," line 42, is referring to Religious Space.

There is the following story among Zen people. About 600 years ago, in Japan, a famous Zen Master Sanko was a teacher of the emperor of the time. A monk asked Master Sanko one day: "Please show me the essence of Zen." Sanko at once replied and said, "Look under your feet!" This reply, "Look under your feet!" means "Where are you standing now?" This tells us that Zen does not exist apart from the very spot where we now stand. For Sanko, there was no place where Zen was not present. He actualized *satori* by way of occupied space. The Zen man who has testified to the truth of Self-nature lives in the realm where time and space are one. If I explain it further, the true Zen man is the master of time and space living at the absolute spot of "here-now."

128

It happens that the phrase "Look under your feet!" from Sanko's famous *mondo*, is much favoured by Zen people in Japan, and is used as a daily motto. Visitors to Zen temples may notice a board on a pillar with this phrase in the entrance hall, giving admonishment to visitors.

As Zen time and Zen space have thus been clarified, the following two lines will follow naturally:

"Where you stand is the Land of Purity. (43)
  Your person, the body of Buddha." (44)

"The Land of Purity" can be simply interpreted as Pure Land or Paradise. Hakuin states that Paradise is nowhere else but "this place now." Usually we are apt to think that an ideal religious world like Pure Land or Paradise exists in some outside world, far and above. Zen clearly declares that Paradise is "this place of here-now." Line 43 corresponds to lines 36 and 38 where Hakuin says:

"Your going-and-returning takes place
      nowhere but where you are;"
"Your singing-and-dancing is none other
      than the voice of Dharma."

What a bold declaration, what joyous tidings!

129

Five hundred years ago, there lived a Zen Master, Ikkyu. He was a son of an emperor but later became a Zen monk. It is well known that when he was young, Ikkyu went through very hard Zen training. He was a good friend of the people in general who loved him and respected him, calling him "Ikkyu-san." He led a free and unrestricted life. He was an unconventional Zen Master who left many anecdotes. In Japanese society of those days, while Zen was accepted by the upper and *samurai* classes, Pure Land Buddhism was popular among the common people. Zen says that Paradise is here in this world. The Pure Land School however claims that Pure Land exists in the western direction beyond ten billion worlds, and that the faithful can be reborn in Pure Land only after their death. This Pure Land teaching is just the opposite of Zen teaching. Ikkyu formed a satirical poem in which he commented on the teaching of the Pure Land School:

"Pure Land is far beyond,
    Ten billion worlds away.
How can I hope to reach there
    With only a pair of straw sandals?"

This poem is often referred to even today. However, now that we have aeroplanes and space ships and do not have to rely on straw sandals, I wonder how the poem could be revised?

The Pure Land School may have its own theological basis and doctrines to support their view of Pure Land. What Zen claims is Religious Space—"here-now." Therefore it is natural that Zen declares that the ideal religious world called Pure Land or Paradise is nowhere else but "here-now" in this world. Enlightened beings, who are the inhabitants of Pure Land are we ourselves. "Apart from your person, there is no Buddha." The characteristic teaching of Zen is clearly represented here.

Recently in Japan there was a great controversy among the Pure Land Buddhist scholars on the subject of whether or not Pure Land should be designated to exist at a certain fixed place.

Zen declares that the place where you stand is it. So to this question, from the viewpoint of religious philosophy, Zen will of course say that it exists at no fixed place. There is no room in Zen for such a question to arise. "Your going-and-returning takes place nowhere but where you are;" and "Your singing-and-dancing is none other than the voice of Dharma."

Although Zen does not discuss the location of Pure Land, Zen does raise a great question when it teaches that the ideal religious world called Pure Land is nowhere else but here in this world.

Aren't we and this world of ours too defiled and too full of sufferings, to declare that "this world is Paradise?" I hope you realize that what is meant is not that this world without any condition is Paradise. Zen teaches that "All beings are primarily Buddhas." In order for one to be able to declare that "Where you stand is the Land of Purity," he has to "Testify to the truth of Self-nature." This actual fact of experience that "One has testified to the truth of Self-nature" is the essential condition in Zen life and gives us Paradise.

In the biography of Kisu, a Chinese Zen Master of the Tang dynasty, there is the following interesting *mondo*. One day Master Kisu walked out of his room towards the kitchen where a few monks were working. "What are you doing today?" the Master asked. A monk answered, "We are working with a hand-mill." "You may mill the grain all right, but never mill the axle," the Master said, and returned to his room. The whole story sounds nonsensical, one might say. Where, then are we to find the significance of the story? Why was it so specially recorded in the text of Zen history?

Are we not crying and shouting everyday, milling the axle together with the grain? Kisu told the monk, "You may mill the grain all right, but never mill the axle." He is asking us to have a firm unshakable basis, deep and serene, at the bottom of our mind, no matter how busily we might run about in a hubbub of our daily life. Whether we are to live in Pure Land or in Hell everyday depends on how we accept this actual world of ours, and how we live in it. We should not "mill the axle," though we may mill the grain.

Zen says that Religious Time and Religious Space are both realized "here-now." The religious personality that lives "here-now" is of course "you," Zen declares. This living religious personality will naturally work out and religious activities be developed at this time.

Joshu has the following *mondo*: A monk came to Joshu and asked, "All things finally return to One, but where does this One return to?"

Everything in the world, every phenomenon in the universe, finally returns to the One Ultimate Truth. Everything in the world finally returns to God. Or we might say that the world of discriminations finally returns to the world of Enlightenment. The monk dared to ask where this Oneness, or the One Absolute Truth should return to. The monk might have had the intention of testing his teacher to see how he would reply to such a difficult and vital question. Joshu, however, quite nonchalantly answered, "When I lived in the district called Seiju, I had a robe made of the famous local fabric." The monk presented a question on the Truth, on God, on Enlightenment—a vital question regarding the highest human life value, but it was the commonest act of purchasing a robe, Joshu says. Most likely the monk did not get the real meaning of Joshu's reply and probably stood aghast at his reply. For Joshu, the commonest act was inclusively his religious activity, his Zen life itself. With Joshu, everything he did was a religious act. He could not live otherwise. In Joshu's mind, there was no such dualistic distinction like religious life and irreligious life. Now we have read every line of Hakuin's Song of Zazen.

The ideal world of Enlightenment in Zen is here-now where the enlightened one develops his daily activities. It cannot exist apart from his actual everyday life. You might even think it too commonplace and uninteresting.

I have come from Japan here, flying over the Pacific to talk on the subject of "Zen.". Were I to tell you that the conclusion to my lecture is "Camellias in the United States are beautiful," would you think it too commonplace and nonsensical? To the contrary I should like to say, "How wonderful it is!"

I now raise my pen in my hand. If we are able to realize that this seemingly insignificant act in the same moment is at once the absolute act penetrating through the whole universe and is directly connected with the fundamental source of life, then we are able to see the secret of creation. Isn't it wonderful? We are much obliged to the ancient Masters who exemplify for us a deep and serene Zen personality. "Mill the grain, but never mill the axle."

In addendum, I have to make one important comment. The ideal Zen personality described in the last part of this Song reflects the religious philosophy of Zen, but the religious ethics aspect of Zen is not well represented. To be a true religious personality, the ethical life based upon religion is to be simultaneously developed. Hakuin did not see the necessity of explaining in detail the ethical aspect of a religious personality in this Song because ethical life is merely a natural expression of the religious personality. This of course does not mean that the ethical aspect is lacking in an ideal image of man in Zen. Hakuin strongly emphasizes the importance of "Training after Enlightenment" in another book he wrote. With much admiration he refers to a verse by an old Master:

"Tokuun is an old rusty gimlet,
    He descends the mountain of Enlightenment
    further and further.

135

Let us hire a sacred fool,
And fill up the well with snow together."

Tokuun was a great sage in an old Buddhist story. In this verse, Sage Tokuun is described as an old rusty gimlet. A new gimlet is sharp and useful. An old rusty gimlet is dull, though still a gimlet. Zen emphasizes the necessity of hard, strict and assiduous discipline to temper and train one's personality.

Additional training is needed, however, for one to go beyond all the discipline to return to "original" humbleness, and then to live an ordinary everyday life without any sign of superiorness. This is called the "Training after Enlightenment," or "Downward Training." It is the training to become like an old rusty gimlet, showing no outward brilliance at all, but keeping it all within.

After much toil and labour one comes to the summit of the mountain. Now he must descend the mountain with utmost care and return to the ordinary daily life on earth. We call such a person the "Great Fool." Rusty he may look, but a true gimlet without doubt. Though ordinary and inconspicuous he may remain, he has a serene, lucid atmosphere around him. Anybody that comes in touch with him will be enveloped in it. This is the ideal Zen personality. People of the East, from olden days, have had the tendency to revere such personalities.

About a hundred and seventy years ago, in a remote country in Japan there was a Zen monk who called himself "Ryokan, the Great Fool." He did not have, or did not care for any social status or ecclesiastic rank, and lived alone in a small mountain sanctuary. He loved playing with the children of the village, and lived a poor and simple life. It was an autumn evening with a beautiful moon above. Ryokan came back to his mountain hermitage to find that all of his few belongings, bowls and dishes, had been stolen. He then made a *Haiku* poem:

> "The moon out the window!
> Left by the thief unstolen."

Does not he somehow resemble St. Francis of Assisi?

Ryokan was one day invited home by his brother. The brother and his wife wanted Ryokan to reprimand their delinquent son. Thus after a long while Ryokan came to see his brother, and stayed there overnight. He, however, did not say a word to reprimand his young nephew, and was about to leave for his mountain hut the next morning. The nephew was lacing old Ryokan's straw sandal when he felt a warm wet drop fall on his hand. He looked up in spite of himself, and saw his old uncle Ryokan looking down at him with tears in his eyes. Ryokan, without uttering a word to his nephew, returned home to his mountain. From that day, however, the nephew changed to being good. I too revere such a personality. "An old rusty gimlet" or a "Sacred Fool" is the name given to describe such a person. Zen says:

"Let us hire such sacred fools and
Fill up the well with snow together."

"To fill up the well with snow"—what an interesting expression this is! If we try to fill up the well with soil, or sand, however small the amount of soil it might be that one carries each time, the well will some day be filled up. If, however, one tries to fill up the well with snow, the day will never come when he can achieve his aim. The ideal man of Zen is such a sacred fool, who keeps on filling-living day in and day out, without being discouraged, even though his efforts may never be rewarded. Hakuin, too, praises such a great fool as the one who leads the ideal ethical life of Zen.

In another booklet of mine I introduced a parable which also illustrates the same ideal of Zen. Let me repeat it here.

A delicate little pigeon once happened to notice a mountain fire burning up many square miles of a forest. The pigeon wished somehow to extinguish the terrible conflagration, but there was nothing that a little delicate bird could do. Knowing well that he could do nothing to help the situation, the bird still could not remain quiet. With irrepressible compassion, he started the flight between the fiery mountain and a faraway lake, carrying a few drops of water soaked in his wings each time. Before long all the energies of the pigeon were exhausted, and he fell dead on the ground achieving no tangible results at all.

Certainly human culture may have achieved great progress in the course of history. Suffering and unhappiness in the human world, however, do not seem to have decreased. The present situation of our world is so full of poverty, distrust, diseases, strife, that there seems to be no end. Hundreds and thousands of great men admired as saints and sages have appeared in the world in the past, and they have devoted their lives for the betterment of the world. Human suffering and unhappiness, however, do not seem to have decreased or ended. Over and over again they repeatedly, thanklessly endeavoured to fill up the well with snow. The true life of Zen is found here, when we all become true Great Fools and calmly and nonchalantly keep on doing our best, realizing well that our efforts will never be rewarded.

Self portrait of Hakuin

Kanwu, a Chinese general

Bodhidharma

利濟群生遠繼之意越後之天塔

目精修千坐䕶摩下入法界意生場

Legend of *Acala Samadhi*

144

Zen Master Daito as a beggar

Avalokitesvara

146

Avalokitesvara emerging from a clam

Mt. Fuji

148

Bamboo broom

149

Zen Master Rinzai

150

年苦行徹骨寒瘦骨如氷絲編雙蘆葦
盡悲六趣輪廻三途苦看歷後來拜此
菩提心惟時萬曆第十庚辰歲新秋吉辰

Sakyamuni Buddha in hard search

151

THE SIX OXHERDING PICTURES
PREFACE

"How should we live?"

"Wherein should lie the true value of human life?"

Since the ancient days many sages and wise men have tried to enlighten us in various ways in regard to these questions. "The Six Oxherding Pictures" is one of these attempts. It accordingly points to the ultimate aim of religious life, and shows us the true picture of faith. In so doing, the author, a Chinese Zen Master of the Sung era, used the simile of oxherding, and developed his talk following the sequence of the very well arranged six pictures. The book thus has a consistent form, and is consequently very interesting to read.

It is my hope that through the kind instructions contained in "The Six Oxherding Pictures" the readers may be able to get in touch with the true spirit of Zen training and its ultimate aim. It is also hoped that from the pictures we may get various lessons as to how we should lead our life and how we should try to realize, step by step, the real meaning of life. The yearning for the "true and warm humanity," which we can only barely glimpse in this warped human world today, can thus be cultivated.

As time and space do not permit, I cannot make any direct references to the "Verses." These Chinese verses, called in Japanese "*Ju*" (頌), have highly poetic and rhetorical expressions. They may appear to be rather complex in meaning, but what they wish to convey may perhaps be understood from my comments following each of the Introductory Remarks (*Jo*, 序).

True Zen is primarily characterized by "Direct Discipline and Direct Enlightenment," i.e. coming to the Enlightenment straight away without going through any gradation. In this sense the Fifth and the Sixth Pictures alone would suffice. The way of true Zen being therefore rather difficult, only those favored with special endowments and special circumstances can master it.

Jitoku, however, wished somehow to make Zen comprehensible to people in general. His eagerness and kindness urged him to come down to the secondary level and explain Zen by way of "gradual disciplinary processes," i.e. coming to the Enlightenment after going through gradual disciplinary processes, so that it can be easily understood by all.

I, also, having originally given these talks to Japanese lay people, have often resorted to very popular explanations including frequent use of expressions from Jodo Shinshu, which may not necessarily be in the spirit of Zen.

The four pictures from the First to the Fourth, explaining the gradual disciplinary process, are generally taken to represent Zen training step by step. They all, however, represent one phase of that which is presented in the Fifth and the Six Pictures. In other words, they are "the gradual in the direct (or sudden)," or one phase of the whole. We should realize that all the pictures thus have two meanings. Consequently, the Six Oxherding Pictures are just One Oxherding Picture, and the One Oxherding Picture is the Six Oxherding Pictures.

Needless to say, there are no such distinctions as enlightenment and ignorance, or gradual steps in Enlightenment or Truth itself. But when one working phase of it is taken apart and treated independently, distinctive stages of enlightenment and ignorance and the gradual steps will come to be considered as existing as such. It was therefore perhaps worthwhile and necessary that such attempts at explaining Zen by way of gradual disciplinary steps were made to guide the ordinary people.

It should therefore be understood that the terms used in the pictures from the First to the Fourth, that is, before the real Enlightenment has been attained, have two meanings—namely, the gradual disciplinary meaning and the absolute meaning transcending all the gradual processes. These terms when only literally interpreted may sound contradictory and inconsistent. I hope therefore that the following explanatory notes may help to clarify the true meaning and guide against the many possible misunderstandings.

EXPLANATORY NOTES
ON THE SIX OXHERDING PICTURES

1. The Oxherding Pictures of Zen

Old Buddhist sutras of the very early periods already have stories of training a wild ox step by step, comparing it to the stages of the "discipline whereby the nature of man who has lost track of the Truth is gradually trained." In the early Sung period when Zen achieved great literary development, several books of this nature were written. They all tried to illustrate by pictures the spirit of Zen training and the spiritual attainment to be expected by such training. These efforts, naturally, must have greatly contributed to the propagation of Zen in those days. Fumyo's (普明) "Ten Oxherding Pictures," Kakuan's (廓庵) "Ten Oxherding Pictures," the "Ten White Ox Pictures" by an unknown author, and the "Six Oxherding Pictures" by Jitoku (自得) were among the most famous.

These various versions naturally reflect the personalities and characteristics of their respective authors, each of whom has his own way of commenting on the pictures. They all, however, are the same in trying in a simple manner, comparing the whole process to that of oxherding, to elucidate the inner progress of Zen training and to explain the ultimate stage at which Zen aims.

Jitoku's "Six Oxherding Pictures" is distinctive in that it adopted what are considered the best from the ideas contained in the "Oxherding Pictures" by Fumyo and Kakuan, further simplified the whole story, and rearranged it into these six pictures.

In any case, it is first necessary, in studying these pictures, to know the connotations of such constituent elements as, the "ox," the "herdsman," "black and white," the "rod," the "circle," etc. The proper method, then, is to get the inner meaning as it develops from one picture to the next, and to try personnally to experience it.

2.   The Mind-Ox

Needless to say, the "Oxherding Pictures" are illustrations which show by consecutive pictures how a wild ox is trained and tamed. The most important questions concerning the pictures are: what kind of ox is this? and what is the inner meaning represented by it?

To give the answer, the ox is "the thoroughly pure and immaculately white Mind-Ox."

The "Mind" of the Mind-Ox is not the ordinary mind. It is the Mind when we say "The True Mind, or the True Nature," which is the ultimate, fundamental Truth of the universe. From ancient days various names have been given to it, such as "The Buddha Nature," "The Truth," "The Enlightened Being," "The True Man," "No-Mind," "The Original Face," "The Sound of One Hand," "Reality," "The True Existence," "The Absolute Being," "The Eternal Being," etc. It is, however, so high and profound in its meaning that there could never be a word that would sufficiently express what it really is. The Japanese Zen Master, Eisai, therefore said: "It is eternally unnamable but, perforce, I call it 'The Mind'." What is represented by "The Mind" here is the religious Truth or the Buddha Mind that would be our ultimate foundation or the abode where we finally find ourselves at peace. The Mind-Ox is thus the "True Ox."

From the standpoint of the Mind-Ox, therefore, it is originally "the thoroughly pure and immaculately white Ox." It is the eternal "Mind-Ox" that could never be defiled in black or go astray in the wilderness. It is, again, the "True Ox" that is identified with the heaven and earth, and is one with all the things on earth.

3.   The Whitening of the Black Ox

Why, then, is the Mind-Ox in the pictures drawn as a black ox? What is the meaning of the colour black?

It means that dark clouds of human attachment, discrimination, delusion, ignorance, etc. cover the eye of wisdom and prevent it from seeing the Truth. This fact is also indicated by the separation of the Mind-Ox and the herdsman.

Buddhism declares that everybody and everything, without any exception, has the Buddha Nature within. This view of man and of the Buddha Nature constitute the essential feature of Buddhism. Truly there is nothing in the

159

universe that is left out of the Truth.

Because of our ignorance we are unable to appreciate the great bliss of being embraced in the Absolute Being, and are unaware of the thoroughly pure and immaculately white Mind-Ox, which is within ourselves. Thus we fancy that the Truth is something that is to be sought after outside of ourselves. This is the reason why the Mind-Ox is shown as a black ox, and the ox and the herdsman are turned against each other.

The reason that the True Ox, thoroughly pure and immaculately white, has to be shown as a white ox of Enlightenment on the one hand, and as a black ox of ignorance on the other, is essentially the same reason that the one absolute personality has to be shown as a man of the true mind which has attained the Mind-Ox on the one hand, and as a man of a deluded mind with the ox turned against him, on the other. In order to make the pictures more impressive and easier to understand, the author used these two symbols in parallel. (In the "Ten Oxherding Pictures" by Kakuan, only the relationship of the herdsman and the ox is pursued, and the change of the color of the ox from black to white is not mentioned. Perhaps he wished to avoid repetition of the same idea.) Thus, if only the whitening of the black ox is described in the pictures, and the relationship of the herdsman and the ox is omitted, there is no change in the inner meaning of the story.

4. The Herdsman

When Sakyamuni Buddha, the founder of Buddhism, saw the morning star glittering in the sky at dawn of the 8th of December, his long ascetic discipline came to an end, and his spiritual eye of Enlightenment was opened. The sutra says that the first words uttered by Buddha on that occasion were: "Wonderful, wonderful, wonderful, indeed! Every being on earth is without exception endowed with the wisdom and virtues of the Tathagata. Only because of one's ignorance and attachments is one unable to come to its realization!" This, as I mentioned before, is an important principle characterizing Buddhism, and represents the Buddhist view of man.

Let me replace here the words "wisdom and virtues of the Tathagata" with the "thoroughly pure and immaculately white Mind-Ox," since they are synonymous. The Buddhist idea of man is, therefore, to realize this "Wonderful, wonderful, wonderful indeed! Every being on earth is without exception endowed with the thoroughly pure and immaculately white Mind-

161

Ox." The Mind-Ox is ever present in each of us, and cannot be otherwise. It is not, therefore, something that should be sought after outwardly.

But, alas, not all of us are awakened to this fact. As is stated in the sutra, "Only because of one's ignorance and attachments is one unable to come to its realization."

We veil the pure and white Mind-Ox, which all of us have in ourselves, with the dark clouds of ignorance, attachments and delusions. This deplorable state is represented by the separation of the Mind-Ox and the herdsman, each turned against the other. Further, the Mind-Ox is shown as a black ox, symbolizing the "ox all covered by delusions, running astray, and turned against the herdsman."

The process whereby the wild ox separated from the herdsman is gradually tamed and finally becomes one with the herdsman, and the process whereby the black ox gradually reveals its original features and becomes white, express the same idea.

In other words, the taming of the wild ox into the real Mind-Ox and the whitening of the black ox both point to the same goal, namely, that we are spiritually awakened and actualize in our person the living of the Buddha's life. Zen calls this "To be awakened to the true Self and to realize the original significance of life."

5. The Tether of Faith

Unlike other creatures, man can reflect and realize how weak and ugly he is. He then pictures to himself the ideal personality, and longs for it. This is where human worth and dignity exist. It is also due to this human characteristic that the more deeply we look into human life, the more strongly we feel nostalgic for that which is true and eternal, that which can be our final home. This is the yearning for our original home.

This feeling of nostalgia and longing buried deeply within us, when guided by good teachers, will grow into true "faith." "Faith" means the aspiration for the joy of awakening in the Eternal and the Absolute, the happiness of losing the self in the Buddha. It is the singleminded longing for the Mind-Ox.

The tether symbolizes "faith." A thought of faith has been awakened in our mind, and the author likens it to the state in which a tether has been fastened to the Mind-Ox which has so far been lost, having gone astray. (Here it is introduced as a dirty wild ox, black in colour.)

I once heard that the English word "religion" etymologically means "to be connected," "to be fastened," or "to get related." I thought this very interesting. God and man are related,

163

Buddha and the ignorant ones are related, the Mind-Ox and the herdsman are related, and here arises faith. The tether is now fastened (a thought of faith is awakened), and for the first time the herdsman and the Mind-Ox are related through the tether. This is the first step toward the man and the ox finally becoming one, for the outer self to be awakened in the inner Mind-Ox and thus to realize its true Self. It goes without saying that the eagerness to seek after the Truth and the zeal to inquire into Reality is encouraged by faith.

6. The Rod of Striving

The rod in the hand of the herdsman indicates the will, effort, and courage which are essential if we are to accomplish anything. If we are successfully to fulfill anything at all, knowledge and desire alone will not be sufficient to carry it through. Courage is required to keep on with the effort for a certain period of time. Much more so with the discipline of our personality. How could we expect to fulfill the aim of getting into the source of life and attaining the joy of spiritual peace without intrepid will and effort?

"The gem, if not polished, shall never sparkle," is an eternal truth. True it may be that we

164

all have within ourselves the true Buddha Nature (Mind-Ox) without exception; but it will forever remain a gem buried in the earth if sincere efforts are not made to break the darkness of our deep-rooted ignorance and to reveal the light of the White Ox.

The rod in the hand of the herdsman represents the force with which to beat and guide the wild ox, which soon tries to run away into the wilderness.

7. A Circle

The fact that all of the oxherding pictures have been drawn in a circle may seen to have no direct connection with the contents of the pictures. This, however, does have a meaning that should not pass unnoticed. The circle may well be compared to a thoroughly polished mirror.

A mirror, thoroughly polished, even though it may have nothing to reflect, is not just a void. It is full of the absolute power to reflect everything. Still it does not have a single stain or dirty spot. Since ancient days, therefore, the mirror has often been referred to as indicating the "True Mind, the True Nature," the "Fundamental Principle of the Universe," the "Great Wisdom of Enlightenment," or the "Life of the

Buddha."

Zen calls this realization of the absolute spirituality "Enlightenment," and the state without this realization "ignorance." Both Enlightenment and ignorance, however, are distinctions made on the surface of our psychology. The True Mind and the True Nature within ourselves, or Spirituality itself, is ever existent regardless of the state of our mind, whether enlightened or ignorant; and all of us, including this universe, are enveloped in it. In other words, whether we realize it or not, we are living right within it. Enlightenment or ignorance is, in this sense, nothing but a shadow reflected on the Buddha Nature, which Buddha Nature, (or our spirituality itself) never increases nor decreases, never is purified nor defiled, but forever retains its lucidity. Thus a circle is used to convey this deep and noble principle, and the process from ignorance to Enlightenment is shown in it.

It is because of this that in the "Six Oxherding Pictures" the Fifth Picture is the basis of the spiritual attainment and is represented by an empty circle. The stages represented by the other pictures are all "shadows" either of ignorance or enlightenment appearing on the Absolute Buddha Nature or Absolute Spirituality.

8. Bibliography

The Six Oxherding Pictures by Jitoku Eki appears as No. 21 in Vol. 2 of the *Zoku Zokyo* (Supplement to the Tripitaka, 續藏經). It also can be found in *Zemmon Shoso Geju* (Verses of Zen Masters, 禪門諸祖偈頌) compiled by Goroho, Shaku Shisho, 五老峰, 釋子昇). In these versions, however, the Introductory Remarks and the Verses alone appear; the pictures which constitute the main part of the book, are missing. The compilers probably omitted the pictures because the Introductory Remarks "well explain the contents of the pictures," or else they did not think it necessary to include them. (For further reading on Ten Oxherding Pictures, see my work in Japanese "十牛圖" (The Ten Oxherding Pictures); Kyoto: Kichu-do, 1963.)

9. Brief Biography of Jitoku

There are two different biographies of Jitoku. One is the inscription in *Jitoku Eki Zenji Goroku* (Sayings of Eki Jitoku, 自得慧暉禪師語錄) in the *Zoku Zokyo;* the other is in the *Zoku Dentoroku* (續傳燈錄), and in *Goto Egen* (五燈會元).

The only point common to these two biographies is that Jitoku was a disciple of Tendo Shokaku (天童正覺). Otherwise they are so different that it is not easy to decide which one to accept. So far, historians have referred mainly to the *Zoku Dentoroku*, and somehow have not given much attention to the inscription in the *Goroku*. According to the *Zoku Dentoroku*, Jitoku died on the 29th of November, in the 10th year of Junki (1183), in the reign of Emperor Koso of the Southern Sung dynasty. His age at death is not recorded. The inscription in the *Goroku* says that he died at the age of seventy on the 15th of December in the 29th year of Shoko (1159), in the reign of Emperor Koso of the Southern Sung dynasty.

In any event, it seems clear that Jitoku was ordained while he was a child, and after studying at various places, came to Tendo Shokaku. He finally was given the Dharma sanction by his teacher, Tendo, and later he presided over various monasteries. Towards the end of his life, he retired to Mt. Seccho, and here passed away in peace.

The First Picture:
AWAKENING OF FAITH

VERSE

One thought of faith is the basis
Which leads one to the way through many
    a rebirth.
Pitiful indeed am I who know nothing of
    the Enlightenment
Piling up one heap of dust over another
    wherever I go.
Wild grasses grow green when the season comes,
The flowers bloom in mad profusion
    day after day.
Longing for the Home and yet not knowing how,
The tears flow and the kerchief is wet.

Introductory Remarks

An instruction is given for the first time by a
    good teacher, and faith is awakened;
A thought of faith once awakened is the basis of
    the way forever.
A spot of white is therefore observed on the ox
    head.

170

The following story is told of Nanin Roshi, a noted Japanese Zen Master of the Meiji period.

Once a young man who was proud of his scholastic knowledge went to see Nanin Roshi at the latter's monastery. When he was led into the Master's room and had taken his seat, the young man was, as is customary, served tea by an attendant. Nanin instructed the monk, "Why don't you pour more tea into the cup?" The attendant monk did as instructed, and when he was about to stop pouring, the Master insisted, "More, more!" The cup was now full to the brim and the monk could pour no more tea into it. The Master, however, still sternly demanded, "More, more!" The young guest could not remain silent, and spoke out, "It overflows, Master!" The Master then quietly said to him, "When one wants to learn anything from others, he has first to empty himself; otherwise there is no room for the teaching to enter. You had better go home now." The young man was ashamed of himself at these words, and with this began sincerely to seek for the Truth.

This story gives us a lesson significant in many respects, and indicates the attitude essential for those who want to lead a religious life and seek after the Truth.

The first step in pursuing the way to religion is to "empty oneself." But this "emptying oneself" does not mean, as ordinarily understood, merely to be humble in one's thinking or to clean out all from the self-deceived mind so that it can accept anything. It has a much deeper and stronger meaning. One has to face the "ugliness and helplessness" of oneself, or of human life itself, and must confront deep contradictions and sufferings, which are called the "inevitable *karma*." He has to look deep into his inner self, go beyond the last extremity of himself, and despair of himself as a "self which can by no means be saved." "Emptying oneself" comes from this bitterest experience, from the abyss of desperation and agony, of throwing oneself down, body and soul, before the Absolute.

It is the keeness with which one realizes one's helplessness and despairs of oneself, in other words, how deeply one plunges into one's inner self and throws oneself away, which is the key to the way to religion. "To be saved," "to be enlightened," or "to get the mind pacified" is not of primary importance. Shinran Shonin, who is respected as one of the greatest religious geniuses in Japan, once deplored, "I am unworthy of any consideration and am surely destined for hell!" This may help explain why those who are in adversity are more accessible to religion than those who are in prosperity.

When one goes through this experience, for

the first time the words of the great religious teachers are directly accepted with one's whole heart and soul. Unconditioned gratitude bursts out as one's spiritual power.

"Faith" also means complete entrusting. To entrust is "to empty oneself." How could one expect to awaken to the true self and attain the real basis of a new life without throwing himself away and emptying himself?

Zen says, "To die once the Great Death." First of all we have to "empty" this vessel called self.

"A thought of faith once awakened is the foundation of the way forever."

A light of faith thus lit will encourage devotion, will stimulate the longing for good teachers, will increase the understanding. The longing and the understanding will then, in turn, deepen the faith and devotion. This is the strange human psychology of mutual stimulation.

"Devotion is by understanding, and understanding is by devotion."

"Devotion and understanding—when these two work together, they form the foundation of the act."

These are utterances of the good teachers from their own experiences. A thought of "faith" is thus forever the basis of accomplishing the way.

The Second Picture:
FIRST ENTERING

VERSE

O my Brother Ox, I ask you,
"How was it that you were so tardy in
    acquainting me with my fault?"
How many kalpas I have wandered away from
    my Home!
What a long time I have been running after
    unrealities!
Each thought is reduced to no-thought,
Each reflection leaves no traces behind it.
Now I start my initiative steps along the way
To the realization of non-doing.

Introductory Remarks

Faith, already awakened, is refined at every mo-
    ment.
Suddenly come to an insight, joy springs up in
    the mind.
First it starts from the top; therefore the head
    is now completely white.

175

That a thought of "faith" has been awakened at the bottom of our mind means that a yearning for something greater than human power has been roused. This is where human beings differ from the rest of the creatures, and show themselves to be spiritually endowed. Once this "yearning" has been roused, human spirituality will never rest satisfied until it reaches the ultimate goal.

"Refining at every moment" is promoted by this inner spiritual power. An ordinary effort, however, will produce only an ordinary result. The hardships the old Zen Masters went through were by no means just conventional.

About two hundred years ago, there was a high ranked priest with a purple robe at a big temple called Daitsu-in in Niihashi, Japan. When he was over sixty in age, he grieved that his spiritual eye was not open, and decided to study under the famous Japanese Zen Master, Hakuin.

The elderly priest was rather busy taking care of his big temple, but his earnestness moved him to visit Hakuin every day for several years. Still he could see nothing. One day he came to Hakuin discouraged. "With such merciful instructions of yours, still I cannot see anything." Hakuin encouraged him saying, "Don't be discouraged so soon. Redouble your efforts and try for three more years. If at the end of the three years, you are still unable to arrive at anywhere, cut my head off!" For three years he disciplined himself most assiduously, but could not get any solution. With might and main all exhausted, he appeared before Hakuin and said, "I cannot see anything." "Can't you! It will be of no use even if you cut my head off. Try once and for all for three more months." So saying, Hakuin, with tears in his eyes, struck down the high ranked priest who was now nearly seventy years old.

The priest could still come to no realization at all in spite of his fervent application. He finally went to Hakuin in bitter tears, "You have given me such kind instructions, but still I cannot see anything due to my heavy *karma*." Hakuin cried back, "Nothing can be done now! No use for you to live any longer!" The priest then said, "Thank you indeed for your kind teaching for these years. With death I will atone for wasting it." Bidding his last farewell in tears, he left the Master with heavy heart.

The old priest passed through the mountain path of Satta. The view from the precipice was beautiful beyond description. He sat down on a roadside stone, and took a last look at the view, lamenting over his fate. In so doing he did not realize that he was soon in deep meditation, forgetting all about himself and the darkness approaching.

Hours passed and the first faint rays of dawn broke through the eastern sky. Absent-mindedly he stood up to cast himself down into the precipice. Just when he was about to step off the cliff, the sun shone out of the clouds. He felt as if electricity ran through his body, and the darkness in his mind all disappeared. Needless to say, he dashed like mad back to his teacher.

This is a story told me in my boyhood days by my own teacher by the fireside. It impressed me strongly. Of course, this story tells of a Zen monk's discipline and experiences. Even today, Zen monks spend years in hard training at monasteries, encouraged by these stories of the ancient Zen Masters. It goes without saying, however, that everybody cannot be expected to go through such training. But we should know that it is no easy task for anyone to establish an unshakable foundation in this human world, full of sufferings and contradictions, and to live the true life, thus attaining the joy of living in the bliss of the Buddha.

Let us reflect on ourselves in the morning, introspect in the evening, and continue the life of "refining," thus purifying ourselves and doing our very best to live in Truth (*Mahaprajna*) and Love (*Mahakaruna*). If I wash my clothes with singleness of heart, the dirty clothes will gain increasing cleanliness in my hands. Does not a flower just cut fragrantly bloom even in the cruel hands which have cut it off?

The mother of Millet, the famous artist, is said to have always told him, "Millet, please never paint for the sake of money, but serve God by your painting."

With a needle, or a spake, or a pen in hand, let us serve the Buddha, working in singleness of heart, and doing the work of non-doing. In truly applying ourselves in this way, we can surely experience real joy.

The Third Picture:
NOT THOROUGHLY GENUINE YET

VERSE

How many seasons are past now since I began
        feeding and watching over you,
    O my Brother Ox!
You are almost ready to be the one in the open
    field, perfectly white.
No longer tempted by the juicy green grass,
You are approaching Mount Himalaya
    [the goal of our journey].
While the right thoughts are collected in Oneness,
The illusive ones are still found mixed
        in the stream.
It is only when all these defilements are
        thoroughly cleansed,
That the true mind is beyond the reach of
        the six vijnanas (modes of consciousness).

Introductory Remarks

An insight has already been attained and is
        gradually refined.
The wisdom is bright and clear, but is not still
        quite genuine yet.
Half of the body is now white.

181

"The Truth is realized in an instant; the Act is practised step by step." This is a well-known old saw by a Zen Master. Here the "Truth" may be simply interpreted as the reason or the principle of things, and the "Act" as our deeds in daily life.

Man has a very complex psychology. It is a cause of human suffering that even though we well understand the "reason," the how or what that should be, we cannot actually carry it out in our actions. Whatever the profound truth we may know, if we cannot attest to it by actually living it, our discipline is just halfway. (So only half of the body is white.)

Kai, a high Chinese governmental official of the Sung dynasty once called on Soshin of Oryo. In the course of the conversation, the official proudly referred to the famous Zen saying, "To be identified with the universe, and to be one with all the things." No sooner than had he spoken these words, the Master struck the table in front of him with a *nyoi** he had in his hand, and then struck a little cat sleeping beside him. The cat was naturally startled, and ran away. The Master quietly asked the official, "Mr. Kai, being identified with all the things, why does the cat

---

* A stick or baton fancifully shaped. It may be of different kinds of material. It means literally "as one wishes or thinks." (*cinta* in Sanskrit.)

run away while the table remains unmoving?"
It is recorded that the official was at a loss as to
what to answer, and could not even utter a word.

Training, if it is to be real, has to be strenu-
ously continued until the "idea and experience"
are all identified. There arises many problems,
however, in actually carrying this out.

The following refers to my own training days
at the Nanzenji Monastery. Near the Monastery
there was Bukai Roshi's private house, which had
been rented out for some time. When the house
was vacated, I was told by Bukai Roshi, my
teacher, to go and clean it.

The house as evacuated by the residents was
in a terrible condition. Somehow I managed to
clean the rooms, but when I came to the toilet,
the condition was even worse. Besides, it happened to be a very hot day in August, and I
could not help hesitating. Unknowingly, my
attitude was as if about to touch something
dreadful.

I was not aware that Bukai Roshi, my teacher,
was behind me. Tucking up his clothes and
bare footed, he pushed me away without a word,
took the damp cloth from my hand and began
to clean the dirty toilet. I stood aghast for a
second. But the next moment I jumped at him,
took back the damp cloth, and started to rub the
toilet, literally forgetting myself. The Roshi,

looking down at me for a little while, said in a quiet tone, "With a damp cloth in your hand, you are still unable to be one with it, being disturbed by the dirty and the clean. Aren't you ashamed of your training?" I shall never forget how shameful I was at his words.

In other words, we are to be one with the situation, transcending all the restrictions. In being happy, if we are happy, in being sad, if we are sad, or if we are sitting, in sitting, we are to be one with it at that very moment and place. Therein exists the real discipline.

It is of course no easy task. But based on our "faith," we have prudently to continue our discipline day and night.

In the early Meiji period there was a great swordsman named Tesshu Yamaoka, the swordsman who initiated the "No-Sword School." He had thoroughly mastered Zen, and was also an outstanding calligrapher.

He used to work on calligraphy, saying that in his lifetime he would copy the Tripitaka in three different calligraphic styles. A friend of his remarked, "It is not easy even to copy it once. What a difficult job have you started, to copy it in three different styles!" "It is not difficult at all," said Yamaoka. "It is not?" the friend asked, surprised. "I write just a page a day," was Yamaoka's reply.

"Just a page a day." What an excellent attitude this is! Delight, sorrow, or the pressure of work, are all accepted, as they are, as the only truth of the day, of that moment. There is a serene peacefulness in this kind of life.

Hui-neng, the Six Patriarch of Zen, taught: "To be one in the Absolute Act," and told us to "Live with the One True Mind, whether going, coming or staying." Is he not teaching us to continue our discipline of taking whatever we face now at this moment in our life as "a page a day"? "Gradual refining," that is, strenuous application, is required in Zen training.

The Fourth Picture:
TRUE MIND

VERSE

The truth that is beyond the realm of
    the six vijnanas,
Is the udumbara flower blooming in the midst
    of a fire.
Thoroughly shorn of all bindings, it stands
    absolutely by itself.
It is pure and free from all attachments;
    there is not a particle of dust in it.
No tethers are needed now,
Where are the man and the animal?
How vastly empty is the world beyond
    the Age of Emptiness!*
The truth which no Buddhas,
    no Patriarchs can ever question.

Introductory Remarks

Delusions no longer prevail;
    just one true mind.
Pure, immaculate, serene;
    the whole body is thoroughly white.

---

* Name of kalpa.

When the training comes to its acme, all the odors of human defilement are thoroughly washed away. A lucidity with neither front nor back will be shining out in shadowless light. Transparency will be prevailing all over. There is the peaceful serenity of transcending everything whatsoever, and at the same time there is felt the absolute stability, unshakable by anything.

"Just one true mind," "pure, immaculate and serene," or "thoroughly white"—these are phrases to express this experience.

I will leave it to the readers to appreciate, as they will, this sort of spirituality. I will just tell a story which may help them understand what is meant here by this picture.

Towards the end of the Tokugawa regime, though the date is not known, in a little village of Kokubu, there was a greatly respected Shin (Pure Land) Buddhist devotee, *Myokonin* in Japanese, called Shoma. In a booklet entitled "The Sayings and Doings of Shoma," which records his devoted life, we read the following:

The Abbot of Shokaku-ji Temple held this devotee, Shoma, in grea favour. One of the monk officials of the temple was rather envious of this, and wished to make Shoma ashamed of his illiteracy. The official took out one of the Jodo Shinshu sutras and asked Shoma, "I have heard that you are a greatly respected devotee. Can

188

you, by the way, understand this Great Sutra?" Shoma immediately replied, "Yes, I can very well." Hearing this, the monk opened a page and said, "Tell me what is written on this page." Innocently, Shoma answered, "It says, 'I will save you. I will save you.' Does it not?" The monk official could not help bowing his head in respect.

In the eyes of Shoma who lived in one True Mind, every character, and everything he saw and heard, was reflected as the Buddha's great compassion.

Also towards the end of the Tokugawa regime, again the exact date is unknown, there was another Shin devotee, a woman called Sono, who lived in the little castle town of Mikawa. She was much respected by the people around. Many invaluable stories of her life of devotion remain. Let me present one of them to you.

Once a Shin follower, after making a long trip, came to see Sono and asked, "How can I get my mind pacified in accordance with the teaching of the Other Power?" She told him, "In the morning and in the evening, whenever anything occurs to you, keep on saying, 'Thanks for everything. I have no complaint whatsoever!'" As instructed, the man faithfully kept on saying from morning till night, "Thanks for everything. I have no complaint whatsoever."

His mind, however, could not get the desired peace. He came to Sono again, all exhausted, and said, "Ever since I received your instruction, I have been doing as you told me. Still I cannot get my mind pacified. What should I do now?" Sono at once replied, "Thanks for everything. I have no complaint whatsoever!" The follower, perhaps because of his assiduous application, was able to open his spiritual eye at these words, and returned home with a great joy.

The genuine faith of Sono has a great strength and sharpness. When the faith of a devotee reaches this stage, the distinction between the Self Power and the Other Power does not exist any longer.

A Zen text called *Hekigan* records the following *mondo* (dialogue):

Bodhisattva Manjusri once asked Sudhana-sresthi-daraka (Zenzai Doji), "Bring me something that does not do any good." Zenzai searched around, but wherever he went, everything he saw and touched was something that would do good. He was unable to find anything that would not do any good. Finally, he had to come back to Manjusri and report: "There is nothing that will not do good."

"Bring me something, then, that will do good," said Manjusri. Zenzai, without hesitation, plucked a blade of grass at his foot and presented it to Manjusri. Manjusri took it up, and showing it to the congregation, said, "This single herb is both able to kill people and to give people life."

The spiritual eye of Zenzai is stainless. Everything he sees and touches is a thing of bliss (One True Mind). When taken up by Manjusri, a single weed is transformed into the Absolute Being (One True Mind) that transcends both ignorance and enlightenment, killing and giving life.

Devotees Shoma, Sono, Manjusri, Zenzai, and the herdsman and the ox are all one in True Mind, are one in spiritual peace. The training has here been completed, we may say.

The Fifth Picture:
BOTH FORGOTTEN

VERSE

No more man, no more ox—no tidings anywhere.
The ancient pathway is abandoned—no friends,
    no souls.
The fog is enveloping everywhere, and
    the rocks are all around in perfect silence.
The mosses cover everything;
    nobody walks the mountain roads.
The mind is empty with no thoughts
    whatever left,
The tracks of the imagination are not
    imprinted in Time.
Where is the old angler with the rod?
The shadowy leaves cover the mountain stream.

Introductory Remarks

Both the man and the Dharma are forgotten and
    the boy and the ox are asleep.
Forever transcending all the forms, there is only
    the great Void.
This is called the Great Emancipation, and the
    Life of the Buddhas and Patriarchs.

Bokuden Tsukahara, one of the greatest swordsmen of old Japan, had three sons. All of them fully inherited their father's genius and mastered the art of fencing. Towards the end of his life, Bokuden wanted to test the ability of his sons. One day, seated in his room, he first called the youngest of the three into his room. The third son walked along the corridor as usual, and flung open the door of his father's room. Something, unexpectedly, fell upon his head. Before it touched him, he stepped back and, quick as lightning, swung his dagger. When he looked down, there was a ball cut in two at his foot. Bokuden had made some trick preparation on the lintel in advance so that the ball would fall down as soon as the door was touched.

"Now return to your room," the father said to the third son. He then called the second son. He, too, quite innocently opened the door, and the ball fell down on his head. He, however, received it in his hands. "Now wait in your room," the father told him.

Lastly, the eldest son was called in. When, however, he was about to step into the room, he intuitively perceived something. Taking down the ball which was dangerously placed on the lintel, he sat in front of Bokuden and said, "I understand you wanted me, Father."

Bokuden now called the other two sons in again. He bitterly reproved the youngest son saying, "You should be ashamed of being upset like that, even for one instant!" He then encouraged the second son to whom he said, "Just one more effort is needed, my son. Apply yourself to further training, and never be negligent!" Finally he turned to the eldest son and acknowledged the maturity of his training, saying, "I am glad that you are now somehow worthy to be my successor."

This story may be a fiction intentionally made up by somebody, but I am not going to go into that here. What a wonderful skill it is to cut the ball falling on his head quite unexpectedly with one swing of the sword! It surely is worth admiration. Bokuden, his father, however, reproved him sternly. Why? The aim of training in swordsmanship does not consist in taking pride in brilliant skill. The swordsman has to transcend all the techniques and get the victory without resorting to the art of fencing. What Bokuden meant was, unless one reaches this stage one cannot be regarded as a true swordsman who has really mastered the mysteries of the sword.

Now, the Fifth Picture, "Both Forgotten," is represented by one circle with nothing in it but emptiness. This may be likened to the attitude of Bokuden's eldest son, which the father condoned.

In "True Mind," the Fourth Picture, "body and mind," "in and out," "reason and act," "man and ox" are all transfused into one. It is like a thoroughly polished mirror, bright and pure. Here one has, of course, reached the acme of training. But how many have ever attained this stage? It should indeed be highly respected.

In the case of art, the artist with a brilliant skill may be an able expert. He cannot, however, be called the superhuman master of the art. To be a real master he has to go through further training to learn how to withhold all the brilliancy of his skill within himself (i.e. to forget all his techniques) and to be refined even to the extent that he does not look extraordinary at all. The ancient wise man, referring to these circumstances, cries, "Break the mirror to pieces!" He demands of us that we break the thoroughly polished mirror, so bright and immaculate, into pieces.

There is a common saying, "*Miso* (bean paste) with the smell of *miso* is not good *miso*. Enlightenment with the smell of enlightenment is not the real enlightenment." All the attainments of the long training up to the Fourth Picture, "True Mind," which have been gained by hard and assiduous efforts, have to be thoroughly cast away. There is to remain no trace of them at all. This is meant by the Fifth Picture, "Both Forgotten."

When Dogen returned from China, where he had studied Zen for years, he was asked, "What kind of noble teachings have you brought back?" He answered, "I have returned empty-handed!" This means that he came back to Japan with nothing whatsoever. This is the state worthy of the utmost respect.

Based on this experience (the Buddha's Life itself), the doctrine of true Buddhism, or true Zen, is developed (to the Sixth Picture).

The Sixth Picture :
PLAYING

VERSE

The impasse is opened and a new vista presents
    itself!
One is back in the six paths of existence.
Everything taking place here is no other than
    the Buddha-life itself.
Wherever one may wander, one is greeted by
    old friends.
This man is like an untainted gem in the mud.
He is like pure gold in the burning furnace.
He saunters leisurely on the path of defilements,
Resting or working as the situation demands.

Introductory Remarks

The source of life is extinguished, and from the
    death he revives;
Assuming any shape according to the conditions
    and playing around in whatever places he
    finds himself in
His personality has been changed, but what he
    does is not different.

199

"The source of life is extinguished" means that everything has been wiped away. Even the holy mind and body of enlightenment are all forgotten. This refers to the Fifth Picture, "Both Forgotten." "From the death he revives," of course, indicates the Sixth Picture, "Playing."

In the Sixth Picture, the word "to revive" is most important. "To revive" is to return once again to the world in which he used to live. Now that he has completed his discipline and attained Buddhahood (the Fifth Picture), he will not stay in the Pure Land, but will stand at the crossroads of the six paths of ignorance, and go right into the flames of hell, like the Bodhisattva Kshitigarbha.

It is said, however, that even the terrible hell fire that burns up everything would not do any damage at all to Kshitigarbha's light clothing, which would just flutter gently, as if touched by a soft breeze. Why is this so?

Because the "I" which has once thoroughly cast away both its mind and body and revived from the "Both Forgotten" is no longer the former I. This body and this life now live anew. In other words, it is the life given by the Great Love of the Buddha. It is the life that is to work as the Buddha's hands and feet. It is, again, the source of creation which will

200

give love and light wherever it goes. It is now endowed with the eternal life and will never be burned or destroyed. He may be in the midst of the vortexes of the sufferings and the joys of the world; still he can accept them as the life of the Buddha, as his graceful presentments. Never would they disturb his believing mind.

A story in one of the sutras of a little pigeon always recurs to me in this connection.

A delicate little pigeon once happened to notice a mountain fire which was burning up so many square miles of a forest. The pigeon wished somehow to extinguish the terrible conflagration, but there was nothing that a little delicate bird could do. Well knowing that he could do nothing to help the situation, the bird still could not remain quiet. With irrepressible compassion, he started to fly between the mountain on fire and a far away lake, carrying a few drops of water soaked in his wings each time.

Before long all the energies of the pigeon were exhausted, and he fell dead on the ground, achieving no result at all. This most impressive story gives us a picture of the "Great Compassion" which exhausts its life with the Four Great Buddhist Vows.*

---

* The Four Great Vows
   However innumerable beings are, I vow to save them;

201

If we were to call what the pigeon did foolish, nothing could be more foolish and useless. But there are saints who would testify that nothing but such a holy, meritless life is the real life worth living; and it is these saints who, in spite of many difficulties, give harmony to the human world and direct it to peace and happiness, however little by little. It is true that the sincere efforts of individuals and nations for peace and happiness were wasted and in vain for many thousands of years, and are still wasted in vain. Yet there is no other way but this for us to follow, and for which we should strive even at the cost of our own lives.

The individual is always connected with the whole. Whenever I am terrified at my own inner conflagration, I am encouraged by this tenderhearted little pigeon. How foolish are we to repeat the same sad mistakes over and over again?

"His personality has been changed, but what he does is not different." This is the saint who, while going through the whirlpools of life,

However inexhaustible the passions are, I vow to extinguish them;

However immeasurable the Dharmas are, I vow to master them;

However incomparable the Buddha-Truth is, I vow to attain it.

makes such a waste of efforts the real aim of his life.

It was right after the war in Japan when living conditions were the worst and the people had lost any peace they may have had in their mind. A poor old blind lady called Nobu, who lived in a corner of a burnt and devasted area, came to worship at a temple, and quite joyously said to the priest of the temple: "Reverend, I have had a light placed near my house." "Did you! Why?" asked the priest. "It is outside my room. My room is in a tenement house in the midst of an alley. The walk is in a terrible condition, and at night it is very dangerous for people to pass through. I have long wanted to place a light for them." The priest was greatly impressed at the answer. I remember that hearing of this story, I was almost moved to tears at the warm-heartedness of the old lady. It made me consider anew what the real value and worth of human life are. So I wholeheartedly appreciate the deep meaning of "Assuming whatever shape according to the conditions," or "To be an uninvited friend."

Flower arrangements by Jowa Hirohata. Born in 1889, Jowa Hirohata trained himself in the arts of flower arrangement and Japanese painting under the guidance of his father who was a master of flower arrangement. Later, as the Head Master of the Koen School, he worked to promote the art of flower arrangement in Kyoto, and was also recognized as an outstanding painter. At present he is a director of the Osaka Flower Arrangement Association. He has been acquainted with the author, Abbot Zenkei Shibayama, for over 30 years.

A FLOWER DOES NOT TALK

Introductory Verse

Silently a flower blooms,
In silence it falls away;
Yet here now, at this moment, at this place,
    the whole of the flower, the whole of
    the world is blooming.
This is the talk of the flower, the truth
    of the blossom;
The glory of eternal life is fully shining here.

Zenkei Shibayama

I

Zen has something serene transcending all things while holding deep wisdom in it. If, however, one tries to get hold of it to see what it is, there remains no sign of it. Zen, above all, abhors intellectual traces, for they are the slaves of discriminating consciousness.

It was in China in the Tang dynasty. Tozan came to see Zen Master Zenne of Kassan, and asked:

"How are things?"

"Just as they are." His answer was as

matter of fact, as plain and simple as it could be. Yet there is a refreshing lucidity in it that strikes our hearts.

"As it is" is "*yomo*"[1] or "*shimo*"[2] in Buddhist terminology, and literally it means "as it is," or "in its suchness." Mere "as-it-is-ness," however, is nature, and not Zen. There must be the fact of self-realization experienced by the individual through his "person" to be Zen. Still it is "as-it-is," and here is the simplicity, serenity, and depth of Zen.

A monk asked Yo of Koin: "What is the essence of Zen?" Yo's answer was: "Choan (Tokyo) is in the east; Rakuyo (Rome) is in the west." To the same question, Sen of Tokusan replied: "One thousand bamboos outside the gate; a stick of incense in front of the Buddha." They show the serenity of the "as-it-is realization," so pure and lucid.

I remember a story about a German mystic, which I think, is quite interesting:

One morning he was taking a walk along the street, and came across a beggar whom he had often met. Without much thinking he said: "Good morning!" The beggar retorted for some reason: "Is there any morning that is not good?"

---

1. 與麼
2. 只麼

At this, however, the German mystic came to a certain realization. The morning is good. It is as plain as that. But here, we see, similar to that of Zen Masters, the wonder of the "as-it-is realization."

A Buddhist of the Pure Land Sect would say, "to be taken in as I am," or "to entrust all." On the surface they sound quite different, but "to entrust" and "as I am" are the same, and they refer to the "as-it-is realization," which in actuality is not easy to attain. Here is, I think, the Zen element seen in the emancipation taught by Pure Land Buddhism.

The serenity of religious experience is obtained after cutting off all the residua of our discriminating consciousness. It is the serenity springing up from the bottom of the heart that has penetrated into the "as-it-is-ness." Here is a verse:

> The serene moon of Bodhisattva
> Saunters in the Ultimate Sky.[1]

The serene moon appears neither in the Sky of Being nor in the Sky of Non-being. It is the

---

1. Sky is 空 (*ku*) in Japanese. The Sanskrit original for *ku* is *sunyata*, which is ofen translated as 'void' or 'emptiness.'

ever shining moon seen only in the "Ultimate Sky."

The Ultimate Sky, however, is the "very realization of as-it-is-ness" that has cut off the duality produced by the discriminating consciousness, which sticks to being and non-being. It is, in reality, none other than the serene moon itself.

II

Once I was urged to explain the difference between "fact" and "truth." To treat this question just intellectually may not be very difficult. From a higher viewpoint, however, we cannot so lightly answer it.

Vimalakirti was a Bodhisattva who had the extraordinary power to invite thousands of Bodhisattvas into a tiny small room without any inconvenience. It is recorded, however, that even with such unusual power, when he was asked by Manjusri: "What is the realization of non-duality that you have attained?" he just remained "silent."

> A cicada sings the whole day long,
> But it is the silent firefly
>   that burns itself with love.

The author of this folk song might, in a sense, have had Zen spirit of Vimalakirti.

It is well known that Engo, the Zen Master who compiled the *Hekigan-roku* (Blue Rock Records) said, commenting on Vimalakirti's "silence": "It is like a peal of thunder!" There is a saying in Zen, "A loud cry does not enter into the ear." Engo, however, must have heard in this "silence" a great sermon echoing throughout the world. True "non-duality," of course is never a lifeless thing concerned with "words and silence."

For my own answer to the question, I threw the fan I happened to have in my hand in front of the questioner, and asked; "Is this fact or truth?" The questioner, however looked dubiously at me and at the fan in turn, and was "silent," perhaps in imitation of Vimalakirti.

If we continue to come and go along the same line and simply engage in conceptual speculations, we shall forever be unable to make a leap into "Oneness"; we shall never be able to live in "God."

Pampass grass in a cylinder—the calm curved line and the dewy tip of the blade appeal to the heart. Is this, indeed, "fact or truth"? "object or mind"? "nature or life"? The answer gives life to the question, and the question gives life to the answer. Thus when all the futile tangles of discriminating consciousness are cut off, the absolute "Oneness" is awakened as "truth" and as "beauty." When this takes place, the truth becomes the fact, and the fact the truth; and they are both functions of the "Oneness."

Mumon, a Chinese Zen Master, sings this out beautifully:

> The cloud and the moon, both the same.
> Valleys and mountains, each different.
> Are they one, or are they two?
> Wonderful! Splendid!

If one fails to grasp the quintessence of "Wonderful! Splendid!" when he is asked, "Are they one, or are they two?" he will be unable truly to appreciate the beauty of a single blade of pampass grass or understand its significance.

III

A little girl sat close to her grandmother before the Buddhist altar, and pressing her little hands together in prayer, she inquisitively asked one morning: "Why are the crane and the tortoise[1] up there in the altar, Grandma?" "My dear," the grandmother replied, "A crane lives for one thousand years, and a tortoise for ten thousand years. Because they are such blessed creatures, they can be there in the altar where

---

1. Candle sticks in the shapes of a crane and a tortoise.

214

it is as beautiful as the Pure Land." The granddaughter looked all the more inquisitively and asked, "What would the crane do after one thousand years, and the tortoise after ten thousand years?" The grandmother answered: "They die naturally. You should know that, my dear." The granddaughter continued: "What will happen to the crane and the tortoise after they are dead?" The grandmother said: "Because the crane and the tortoise are blessed creatures, they will go direct to the Pure Land when they are dead." The granddaughter persisted: "What would they do in the Pure Land, Grandma?" "What a dull child you are! They would be candle sticks in the Pure Land." The grandmother's answer sounded laboured, but the innocent child nodded her little head contentedly.

This little story has in it something which we cannot just lightly laugh off. Among Zen *mondo*[1] there is a question: "What is it ultimately?" The replies to this are interesting: "Willows are green and flowers are pink." "A short person is short; a tall person is tall." "The moon is in the sky; water is in the jar." Reading these answers by Zen Masters, we feel that we should not, perhaps, laugh at the grandmother who answered that "they would after all be candle sticks."

---

1. Zen questions and answers.

Dogen was asked, when he returned home after completing his hard-earned studies in China, "What great Buddhist teaching have you brought back?" His well-known reply was: "I have horizontal eyes and a vertical nose."

There is a German saying: "Faith is a decision." This is a significant remark from the Zen viewpoint. This is like a person who asking himself why, and why, drives himself further and further up a one thousand foot pole, and upon reaching the top, makes a leap. This leap in Zen is when "attainment" is identified with "faith" as an actual, concrete fact in his religious experience.

"Willows are green, and flowers are pink." In Zen, this is not a comment on willows or flowers. "My eyes are horizontal and my nose is vertical," is Dogen's "attainment" and "faith"; he is not talking about eyes and nose. As regards the question, "What is it ultimately?" if one once penetrates to the ultimate origin, the object, as it is, transcends the realm of object. Here, the beauty of Zen is that it works out as "truth" and as "fact."

IV

A monk asked Zenne, a Zen Master who lived at Kassan: "How is the state of Kassan?" This is a question asking about Zenne's spiritual serenity, about his Zen attainment. The Master's answer, however, was a beautiful verse on lofty mountains and deep valleys:

> A monkey with a baby[1] in its arm,
>> Returns beyond the green hill.
> A bird with a flower in its bill,
>> Flies down before the blue rock.

---

1. "Baby" here signifies some kind of fruit.

If, however, this beautiful verse is not just a description of lofty mountains, but is Zenne's Zen and his spiritual attainment, where in the verse should we see it?

From olden times Zen monks left a great many *mondo* which sound like the exchange of beautiful verses. I will give an example from the *Hekigan-roku*.

One day, Chosa came back from his mountain walk and was met by a monk at the monastery gate. The monk asked, "Where have you been, Master?" This, of course, is a question concerning the "Mind"; he is not asking about any spatial place. Chosa, however, quite innocently answered, "I have been on an outing." The monk put a second searching question to the Master, "To what sort of place did you go?" Chosa was utterly innocent and amiable in replying. His answer in beautiful verse was:

> First I left following the fresh verdure;
> Then returned pursuing the
> falling blossoms.

"So the spring was in all its glory, wasn't it?" the monk went on. The Master's reply gets even more exquisite: "More beautiful it was than the lotus heavy with autumn dew."

Seccho, another Zen Master, commented on

this *mondo* in a verse, which is also an excellent work of art:

> The whole earth is devoid of dust,
> Who would not be awakened?
> First he left following the fresh verdure;
> Then returned pursuing the
>   falling blossoms.
> A crane perches on a bare
>   winter tree crying;
> A monkey cries on the ancient
>   ruin in the wilderness.
> Inexpressible meaning of Chosa—Ah!

The couplet of "crane and monkey" has been admired as a real living phrase, not even yielding to Chosa's "falling blossoms and fresh verdure."

The serenity of Zenne, the exquisiteness of Chosa, and the loftiness of Seccho—what is it that is hidden behind these Zen Masters' sense of beauty and their artistic tastes? Only those who know it know.

If one fails to see the lively "Person" in the beautiful verses as they are, the verses will remain to be verses but will never be Zen. They could be works of art, but are not life. The "beauty" of Zen is the inner power that unites nature and life from within.

V

One day Fugan of Nansen was working on the mountain with a sickle. A monk came up the mountain path and asked, without knowing to whom he was talking: "How can I get to Mt. Nansen?" The Master raised his sickle in front of the monk, and said: "I paid 30¢ for this sickle." The monk retorted: "I did not ask you about the sickle." "What, then," queried the Master, "did you ask me?" The monk repeated: "How can I get to Mt. Nansen?" The Master said: "Oh, yes! This cuts well!" Even such

221

kind instruction cannot be appreciated by those who do not understand it. Zen is not a chasing after the "shadow" of the truth which is separated from the self. Apart from this absolute "spot" here-now, where can we find the true self? To the monk, who did not really know where to look, the kind instruction of Nansen was but a pearl cast before swine.

Nehan of Hyakujo had an even more unique way of guiding monks. From morning till night he kept on saying, "Work for me on the field, and I will teach for you." He thus made his disciples work on the field all the time; but he did not seem to be prepared to give any lectures or sermons. Finally the monks, not able to stand it any longer, went to the Master and asked: "Would you please be gracious enough to give us an edifying sermon?" The Master's unwavering reply was: "Work for me on the field, and I will teach for you."

Several days passed, and the impatient monks went to the Master again and urged: "Please give us a sermon." This time, he quite readily agreed to do so.

After a while all the monks gathered together in the hall. The Master quietly appeared before them, walked up to the pulpit, spread out both his arms, and without a word immediately

returned to his room. Too late! Can't we see the monks standing aghast?

If we work with sweat on our forehead, aren't we, as we are, in the bosom of the "Absolute?" To give abstract sermons is after all to chase after the "shadow."

When we open our mind-eye inwardly towards our true self, every movement and every act of ours is directly the way of Zen. Some have explained Zen Enlightenment as "to return to the work of the actual living person itself." This is a very significant remark.

"The dignity of labour"—this well-known phrase describes "a person who accepts and lives the truth." If this is interpreted simply morally, the deep religious aroma of the words will be lost.

VI

Joshu is the famous Zen Master who left us the *koan*,[1] "*Mu.*"[2] He continued with his Zen training until the age of 85, and lived till he was 120 years old. He was a most brilliant figure in the Zen world of that time. It is said that his lips emitted light. The following story is from his biography.

---

1. 公案, a Zen "problem."
2. *Mu* 無, is a special Zen term which points to the essence of Zen teaching. It is translated as "nothingness," but it has nothing to do with mere negation, or affirmation.

One morning Joshu was walking in front of the Zen Hall, treading on the deep-drifted snow. He accidentally lost his footing and fell in the snow. He cried out loudly, "Help me out! Help me out!" A monk heard him crying, came running, raising snow clouds, and instead of helping the Master out of the snow, "threw himself in the snow too." That is, the monk laid himself down in the snow like the Master. Joshu, who could very well have given the monk a blow of his stick, quite calmly returned to his room.

Now, did this monk help the old teacher out or not?

Dr. Daisetz T. Suzuki says in his *Zen Buddhism and its Influence on Japanese Culture:*

"Zen undertakes to awaken Prajna found generally slumbering in us under the thick clouds of Ignorance and Karma. Ignorance and Karma come from our unconditioned surrender to the intellect; Zen revolts against this state of affairs."[1]

In the world of the intellect, which is called "common-sense," what the monk did has to be judged mad. In the Zen world, however, logical behaviour is not accepted as the only truth. At the same time, however, Zen will not say that

1. D. T. Suzuki, *Zen Buddhism and its Influence on Japanese Culture*, Kyoto: The Eastern Buddhist Society, 1938, p. 5.

truth exists outside logical behaviour. Zen is
trying to say that there is a perspective of a quite
different order; for truth, as the source of creativity, is ever shining at the bottom of logic.

The Master's mind and body are the monk's
mind and body, the monk's mind and body are
the Master's mind and body. Here the "transcendental true wisdom" *(prajna)* shines out penetrating both self and others.

A flower in a little vase has a religious depth
and loftiness of its own, but it can be appreciated
only when one is rooted in the *prajna* understanding of "throwing himself in the snow too."

The artistic character of Zen may be the
aroma which originates in this depth and loftiness.

VII

"An ordinary man entrusts himself; a wise man to the object." This is an extract from a talk by an old Zen Master.

Basically, religious attainment has a kind of passive tranquillity. It has even been criticized by some people as being negative. This passive expression of "entrusting oneself to the object," however, shows a living attitude based on a firm conviction, which is not negative at all. On the contrary, "I myself become the object," is a lucid, active attitude.

A Zen personality, as creative subjectivity, always expresses itself through the *samadhi* of becoming the "object itself." "To cast oneself away" is "to become the object itself"; with the whole of one's being one gives life to the object.

A monk asked Joshu: "I have long heard of the great stone bridge of Joshu. Coming here, however, I have found just an ordinary log bridge." In Joshu, where the Master Joshu lived, there was a famous stone bridge; hence this question. It goes without saying that the monk was only overtly making use of this theme, but was not in fact asking about the "stone bridge itself."

Joshu replied: "You see the log bridge, but you are unable to see the stone bridge." The monk said: "Then what is the stone bridge like?" Joshu answered: "It lets pass over it dogs and horses." Joshu was the "personality of the object itself" that let pass over it dogs and horses.

Later, another monk came to Joshu and asked the same question: "How is the stone bridge of Joshu?" It is recorded that without hesitation Joshu said, "Go ahead and pass over!"

"The personality that has become the object" has no traces of dualities such as truth and falsehood, you and I, subject and object, etc. There is no distinction between the stone bridge and Joshu. The abstract is at once the concrete.

230

"Beauty is the will to affirm realities." This, I understand, is the first proposition of aesthetics. Apart from the living personality of "becoming an object," however, this is idle and false talk.

Dogen has an excellent phrase: "To be testified to by the ten thousand things (everything)." What is presented here is the Zen life of "Body and mind having dropped off; having dropped off body mind!"

In the world of the Absolute, an object and a man are not regarded as two separate things. The logic of Zen has the uniqueness of basing itself on, and developing itself from, this "Oneness." A flower on a twig is I-myself embraced by the Absolute, and an ear of millet is I-myself breathing in the divine light. Hence Zen says, "A grain of wheat is as heavy as Mt. Sumeru," and "Out of a blade of grass, a golden Buddha 60 feet high is produced." At the bottom of the object, at the bottom of the action, there is, so to speak, deep philosophy and the "Person."[1]

---

1. 人 (*nin*) in Japanese. It refers to the personality of the enlightened man living Zen.

VIII

I like the word "truth" very much. Bankei, a Japanese Zen Master, said that everything could be settled by the "unborn."[1] I myself think everything could be settled by one word "truth."

Several years ago I made a free translation of the *Prajna-paramita-hrdaya-sutra* for the young people in Japan. The word which troubles everybody in this sutra is "*sunyata.*"[2] I, too,

---

1. 不生 (*fusho*) in Japanese.
2. Refer to p. 4.

really racked my brain in translating it. I thought about it over and over again, and finally decided to translate it as "truth." I actually used the three characters 一真実 meaning "One Truth," and read them *makoto* in Japanese. Of course, I was well aware of the many possible objections to this translation.

In China in the Tang dynasty, there was a great Zen Master named Baso. One day he asked Yakusan, one of his disciples, "What is your understanding these days?" "All the skin has dropped off, and there is just One Truth," was Yakusan's famous reply. I, however, did not directly refer to this *mondo* in using the words "One Truth." I rather prefer the following *mondo* of Bokuju:

In China in the Tang dynasty, a high governmental official—the governor of the district—came to see the Zen Master Bokuju. Bokuju stood up, and pointing at the chair on which he had been sitting, asked, "What do you call this?" The governor said, "I call it a chair." No sooner had the governor finished answering than the Master roared at him: "You good-for-nothing fool!"

On another occasion, a learned and respectable scholar monk who had lectured in front of the emperor and had been given a purple robe, came to see Bokuju. Bokuju lost no time in starting a *mondo*. Pointing at the visitor he asked, "What is this?" Like the learned scholar that he was, he replied, "Form!" Bokuju, however, saying, "You liar and miscreant!" pushed the scholar out of the room and closed the door. ("Form" is used as opposed to "mind," and may be taken as the "existence with a form which eventually will perish.")

It is true that Bokuju was a rather eccentric Master who spent his life in a hermitage in a remote countryside making straw sandals and never accepted the abbotship of any big temples. But it is also true that he was a great Master whose training had been fully matured. Why was he not satisfied with "straight" answers, and why did he always shout at those who offered them?

Seeing the chair, he must have seen that which "transcends the form." For this "something" which Bokuju saw beyond the form, I would like to use the word "truth."

Of late, people frequently talk about historical views. I, however, am much more inclined quietly to look at so-called history from that something which transcends history.

IX

Once again in the Tang dynasty in China, there was a Zen Master called Sekito (stone head), so called because he constructed a hut on a big flat stone which he found in a mountain, and lived there. There is the following anecdote about him: One day a young monk in training came to see him. Sekito asked: "Where have you come from?" The monk answered, "From Kosei, Master." Sekito then said: "In Kosei, the famous Zen Master Baso lives. Have you ever seen him?" "Yes, I have," the monk replied. The Master, pointing at a big piece of firewood nearby then asked a most extraordinary question, "Does Master Baso look like this?" Unfortunately the monk, with whatever Zen ability he might have had, was no match for Sekito. He blinked his eyes, and could not utter a word.

Baso was a venerable Master revered as the "Great Teacher." What convincing reason did Sekito have to compare the Great Teacher Baso with a piece of firewood, and ask "if he looked like it?" We have to say that it is utterly absurd to ask such a question.

Let me ask here, however, if we are not repeatedly making mistakes by differentiating beauty and the expressions of beauty, matter and mind, you and I, space and time, all the while considering outselves to be logical.

The spiritual eye of Sekito was directed to a higher realm where these dualities are interfused. In his so-called "extraordinarily absurd" remark, the "One Truth"—which envelopes truth, good and beauty as one—is shining.

This *mondo* has its sequel: The astonished monk returned all the way back to Kosei, met the Great Teacher Baso, and told him of the story. Hearing it, Baso asked, "Was the firewood you saw big or small?" "It was very big," the monk answered. "You are a man of great strength," was Baso's unexpected reply. " Why, Master?" queried the monk, at a loss as to how to take it. Baso, it is recorded, then said: " You have brought here such a big piece of firewood all the way from Sekito. You surely are a man of great strength, aren't you?"

Baso asked the monk if it was "big or small," but what he was talking about was not the firewood. Needless to say, it was a remark of Baso's great compassion trying to awaken the monk to the "Absolute," which cuts off big-and-small and transcends subject-and-object. Pitiful was the incapability of the monk to penetrate such a kind teaching.

Now, putting the Zen *mondo* aside, let us look around our world. There are indeed many artists, religionists, politicians or social reformers of "great strength" who carry around somebody else's firewood; but those who see into what is true and calmly carry their "own treasure" are not very many.

X

In the Tang dynasty, there was a famous Zen
Master called Tanka. Because his spiritual endowments were so rich and outstanding, his
teacher Baso gave him the name "Tennen"
(natural). "Tennen" or Tanka was a real Zen
genius.

One severe winter day, he visited the temple,
Erinji, in the capital. It was a very cold day,
piercing and unbearable. Without hesitation he
walked into the main hall, took the wooden
Buddha statue down from the altar, and immediately started a fire, using the Buddha statue as

239

the firewood. He was audacious enough to enjoy the warmth of the fire even turning his back to it. The resident priest hearing of this, breathlessly ran out of his room, and rebuked Tanka for his extraordinary behaviour.

Tanka, however, was not frightened at all. Deliberately poking the fire with his stick, he said, "Don't get so excited. I am trying to get the Buddha's *sarira*[1] by burning this Buddha." The resident priest, whose Zen ability was not quite sufficient, could not get the true meaning implied in this remark addressed to him. He thought Tanka was just making fun of him, and said, "How can you get the *sarira* out of the wooden Buddha?" "Do you say it has no *sarira*? If it has no *sarira*, then it is just a piece of plain wood. All right, I might as well burn the Buddhas on the side too." So saying, he took the two side Buddha statues down, and burnt them too.

The sequel to this story is rather horrible. Contrary to the general expectation that the Buddha's retribution should be inflicted on Tanka who had burnt the Buddha, it was the resident priest who had rebuked Tanka and tried to stop him from burning the Buddha who was punished. For, according to the record, he became hideously

---

1. *Sarira* is the remains of a cremated Buddha or a holy being, often bones or pebble-like matter.

disfigured. His eyebrows fell off and his face became contorted. Does this mean that it was Tanka, and not the resident priest, who was with the true Buddha? Anyway, I will leave this subject off here.

From olden times, Zen Masters with their profound lucidity would smash or otherwise destroy any idol. The iconoclasm of Zen thus issues immediately from the source of free creativity. We can see here the robustness of a sound man of nature. He is the master of himself wherever he may be. He expresses his life in every movement of his hands and feet. A splendour free from any fixed ideas is exhibited here. True beauty, or the life of art, when it comes to this point, is finally interfused into, and becomes one with, Zen.

Recently, flower arrangements in Japan are predominantly of a new style, indiscriminately using painted wire and coloured roots. Of course, this too, can be an expression of beauty in its own way. If, however, beauty is formalized as a norm, there is the danger of its life becoming frozen. The life of true beauty is seen in the creativity of a free, natural man, and this creativity shines out from the depth of his whole-hearted activity in which he keeps on demolishing everything idolized.

XI

Here again is another story taken from the Sung dynasty in China. Shigo, a Zen Master who later lived at Mt. Monju in the Jotoku district, was born in a family whose occupation was butchery. At first Shigo himself worked as a butcher everyday. However, either he had been born with special endowments, or else he had been struggling with his inner spiritual anguish. One day, at the moment he slaughtered a wild boar, all of a sudden he had the exquisite experience of being one with the universe, of

transcending himself and the world. In other words, his spiritual eye was opened to the "Absolute Dimension." He then quit his job, came to Mt. Monju, and was allowed to study Zen under Shindo. The verse recorded as the verse of his Enlightenment is quite wonderful:

> Yesterday, the heart of a demon,
> This morning, the face of a Bodhisattva.
> A demon and a Bodhisattva—
> No distinction is existent.

A flower on a twig in the field has the grace of nature. Though it has natural beauty, it cannot be an art. Placed in a vase in the alcove by some human hand, the same flower, the self-same twig it might be, would leap out of its natural beauty, and give rise to a form of newly created beauty, a beauty of art. That is, it becomes a creative work of art, and at once moves the soul of those who see it, giving it a cultural worth. (Of course there might be those unfortunate cases in which the human hand destroys even the original natural beauty of the flower.)

It might be interesting to interpret Butcher Shigo's Enlightenment like this.

It is well said indeed that "Yesterday, the heart of a demon; this morning, the face of a Bodhisattva." Needless to say, a demon means a devil, ignorance, and ugliness; while Bodhi-sattva means a Buddha, Enlightenment and beauty. If, however, we conclude that there is from the beginning no artistic beauty in a wild flower of the field, and dualistically discriminate wild flowers and arranged flowers, then we are already in the wrong path of ignorance and delusions.

A butcher and a Buddha's disciple, nature and art, they are neither one nor two. Here we come to the inexpressible, and from this exquisite point true religion and true art shines out with eternal brilliance. Of this, Shigo declares, out of his religious experience, "A Bodhisattva and a demon—no distinction is existent."

Zen man Rikyu once said, "In arranging flowers for a small room, one flower, or two, of single colour, is to be lightly arranged." I like this remark very much. The word "lightly" is not light at all; in this one word we can detect his spiritual eye of art with its deep Zen insight. Not only that, we can further see, in this one word, the "spirit of subjective beauty" which will freely work out and develop itself in different kinds of flower arrangements, whether for a big hall, for a show window, a "traditional" arrangement, or a "de-formed" arrangement. The secret of vivid creativity in art is to be found hidden here; or would you say that I am over-estimating Rikyu?

When it comes to this point, there is no distinction between religion and art.   They are identified; they are neither one nor two.

It was while I was still a training monk at the Nanzenji Monastery.   One day, a follower of my teacher, Bukai, brought a picture of a skull to him, and asked him to write a panegyric on the painting.   Preparing the black ink at my teacher's order, I was rather curious as to what kind of comment he would write for such an ugly skull.   After a while he took the brush, and wrote down in Chinese: "If one knows that ice turns to water, beauty and ugliness should both be beautiful."   He said smiling, "Well, the skull should be revived by this, shouldn't it?"   I still remember these words with his smile.

The artistic life of Zen exists where "Beauty and ugliness are both beautiful."   Ordinary conventional "beauty" is no other than an enslaved prejudice.   Here, indeed, is the secret of "Beauty and ugliness—no distinction is existent."

XII

The "Way" is pronounced in the Japanese language as *michi*, and *michi* has the meaning of "abounding." Therefore, they say it means that the "Way" is always abundant everywhere. In olden days, if one scooped water, the moon was in his hands; today, if one plucks a flower, fragrant is his robe. Pines are green and flowers are heavy with dew. Truly, the "Way" is a-bounding any time, anywhere.

There was a monk in training under Dogo called Soshin. He was a dear, sincere young monk worthy of his name.[1] He had become distressed, and felt it to be beyond endurance. Since the time he had come to the monastery for training, his teacher Dogo had not given him, even once, any instructive sermon or appropriate guidance.

One day Soshin, who could not stand it any longer, went to his teacher and asked: "Ever since I came to this monastery, you have not given me your gracious teaching even once. What could be the reason for this?" To this, the Master gave the least expected reply, for he said, "Why? Ever since you came to my monastery, I have not, even for one moment, neglected to teach you." "What kind of teaching have you given me, Master?" Soshin asked. "Well, well! If you bring me a cup of tea, don't I receive the cup? If you serve me meals, don't I eat them? If you greet me with your hands pressed, don't I return your bow? How have I ever neglected to give you guidance?" Soshin, listening to this, hung his head deep, and for a while could not utter a word. Suddenly the Master's roaring cry, as if abusing him, fell on his whole being: "When you see, see it direct! If a thought moves, it is gone!" At this, Soshin uttered an unintentional cry "Oh!"

---

1. Soshin (崇信) means "to revere and believe."

and prostrated himself before the teacher, in tears, whether of joy or sorrow he himself did not know.

The guidance of Kyogen was even more direct and intense, I should say. A monk came to see him while he was drinking tea. He poured tea into another cup, and offered it to the monk. When the disciple was just about to take it, the Master withdrew the cup and demanded: "What is this?" Naturally the disciple was not able to give him any answer at all. Without a word Kyogen struck the disciple down. The pity indeed was the monk's inability to appreciate the "Way" which is "abounding" even in a cup of tea. We, however, have to remember that untold hardship and austere discipline is required for anybody to acquire as his own the Way as truly abounding. For a Zen man, "Everyday mind is the Way," is his life's cry.

I have heard that the founder of the Misho School of Flower Arrangement said the following: "A seat is a flower, a vase is a flower, a board and a stand are flowers, water is a flower, grasses and branches are of course flowers, the arranging person is a flower, and the mind, too, is a flower." This is a remark which the Zen man cannot just pass over.

When one's spiritual eye of "beauty" is open and one realizes that seeing, hearing, standing

249

or sitting are all nothing but flowers, then for the first time flower arrangements can be the Way and will have religious depth. It is on this basis that true flowers are to be freely and creatively arranged.

XIII

This is an anecdote about Yakusan, who is famous for his *koan* "non-thinking."[1]

It was perhaps in his later years and probably the mid-autumn season.   He was walking along the mountain lane one evening.   Suddenly the clouds disclosed the harvest moon, brilliant and serene, and Yakusan burst out with a loud laughter "Ha!" This great cry, however, echoed all around, even to the villages ten miles away from the mountain.

---

1. 非思量 (*hishiryo*) in Japanese.

The next morning, people were inquiring "What was that strange cry we heard last night?" Nobody knew the master of the cry. The inquiry spread around and finally reached to the monks on the mountain, and for the first time they knew the "it was Yakusan's cry at the moon!"

This is, after all, just a nonsensical story, that is, that "he uttered a cry sighting the moon which had suddenly broken through the clouds, which cry echoed to the distance." Why, then, was it especially recorded in the orthodox text of Zen history entitled *Keitoku Dentoroku* (The Transmission of the Lamp), to be so significantly transmitted down to us today?

I am not going to discuss this further here. But, at the word "non-thinking" we think of logical philosophy, and at the cry "Ha!" we conclude that it is just an emotional exclamation. Here might be "something" that blurs our lucidity and prevents our freedom, and we have once and for all to break through it.

Zen points to the "Absolute" shining at the bottom of logic and philosophy, transcending the intellectual discrimination of "non-thinking" and "one cry," and Zen demands us to take hold of this "vividly alive person." Both "non-thinking" and "one cry" are after all shadows lingering on the "one true person," aren't they?

253

Zen is neither conception nor philosophy. It is the living fact, and apart from the "Person himself," all is idle and silly talk.

There is another anecdote about Yakusan. For some reason he had not given any lectures to his monks for a pretty long while. The head monk came to him and asked: "Everyone has long been looking for your instructions. Could you please give us a lecture?" "All right, ring the bell and call the monks together," Yakusan answered.

Soon, the bell resounded in the monastery grounds. When a host of his disciples gathered around his seat, Yakusan simply stepped down from his seat in silence, and immediately went back to his room.

The amazed head monk followed Yakusan to his room, and remonstrated with him saying: "You said that you would give a lecture for the monks. Why did you leave without a word?" Quite calmly, Yakusan replied: "For the study of sutras there are scholars of sutras; for the clarification of doctrines there are theologians. I am a Zen monk, and why in the world do I have to be blamed by you like this?"

The head monk (who had glasses made of radish cut into round slices with holes) was, unfortunately, unable to grasp Yakusan's true spirit.

"Non-thinking," "one cry" or "coming down from the seat"—when these are all cast off, there is the personality which is the source of all acts and deeds. Zen calls it the "Man of the Way relying on nothing," or the "True Man of no title." Let us once realize this True Man of no title, and then our spiritual eye will be opened to truly see all acts and deeds.

Today people talk so much about independence or freedom in various ways. If, however, they do not come to the above realization, this will mean that their "freedom" will end in merely being passively released from something. It will fail to have the positiveness of being able to declare that "freedom is creativity."

XIV

In a Zen text which I keep at hand, the following *mondo* is recorded: One day a high governmental official came to see Tohei. As soon as the official was shown into the Master's room and had taken his seat, Tohei greeted him with a question: "What colour is the wind?" To this unexpected question, the official could not utter a word in reply. Tohei then addressed the question to his monk disciple who happened to be there: "What would you say" This monk was apparently not a common sort of a fellow,

256

for he immediately lifted up the long sleeve of his black robe in front of the official's nose, and said, "Well, let us spread this in your office!" Did he mean "Look at this colour of the wind!"? Unfortunately it is not recorded how the governmental official reacted to this. At the unexpected question "What colour is the wind?" we do not have to stick to the wind or to colour.

We are slaves of the discrimation between yes-and-no, subject-and-object, and slaves to the various names. Tohei's question was his compassionate "thirty blows" trying to save us from this miserable slavish condition by crushing our discriminating consciousness. True freedom, or true creativity, shines out only when we break through this barrier.

The monk lifted up the long sleeve of his black robe and answered in place of the official, "Let us spread this in your office!" But I will not pursue this question of colour any further here.

What I would like to spread, not only in the office, but everywhere in the world where people live, is neither the black robe, red carpet, nor blue cloth. Human truth with which we face "God" and Buddha, this alone I would like to spread all over.

True art, or true religion, should be the

spiritual motivation to awaken deep humanity at the bottom of reality.

Recently at the bottom of the modern people, who are tired and afraid under the pressure of modern culture, nostalgia for missing humanity seems to be gradually awakened. This nostalgia may not be satisfied by political reformation, improvement of economic systems, or diplomatic negotiations alone; it seems to be more deep-rooted than that.

Is it not the time now for us quietly to re-study the deep truth of religion, with our new thinking and viewpoint of this age?

Religion has now to cast off all the dregs of history, and return to its original genuineness. It must provide a clear answer to the nostalgia for humanity stirred in our mind.

XV

Ummon was a great Zen Master who was active towards the end of the Tang dynasy and the beginning of the Five dynasties period. He is also famous for his many *mondo* on the subject of time, by which he showed his Zen attainment.

A monk once asked him: "How should I be prepared in order not to waste time during the 24 hours of the day?" "From where have you brought out such a question?" was Ummon's unforeseen reply. Naturally the monk had to confess: "I cannot at all understand what you say."

Prior to this, Ummon had given his famous sermon to his monks: "Every day is a good day." He did not live in the world where time and self had to be discriminated. He must have seen and acted in quite another world.

Joshu, a Zen Master who is famous for his *koan*, *"Mu"* (nothingness), also declared: "You are being employed by the 24 hours; I am fully employing the 24 hours." He is thus admonishing his monks always to be the master of time.

The fool who asks: "How could I avoid wasting 24 hours" must surely be wasting time. He must be one who has lost sight of his true self, who is driven by the devil called history.

"An adept, though he may look easy, is never dull," is a wise saying. For men like Joshu and Ummon who were complete masters of time whether coming or going, sitting or lying, such questions as this would have been so exasperating that they probably would not have been able to keep from shouting, "You blockhead! See under your feet!" They had no time outside themselves; for them there is no time apart from the fact of their living. For them, time is something that can in no way be wasted. We cannot help envying them.

Daito, the National Teacher, gave the following mid-term (15th June) sermon:

"We know day and night as measured by time; and season measured by days. This is our common understanding. However, if heaven and earth have not yet been separated, and if distinctions have not yet come into existence, is this day to be called mid-term, or not?"

It is our common (dualistic) understanding to measure time according to some standard set relatively. For one, however, who as the master of time has cast off all discriminating consciousness and lives in Absolute Oneness, no relativistic time exists. He would ask: "How should this day be called? How should it be named?"

The truth of eternal life would not care whether the new year might come in January or in December. Such truth pays no attention to divisions made by man, who cannot help regarding time as a separate stream outside himself. In the Zen man's view of time there is bold transcendence, imperturbable by anything. Neither new year nor year end can touch it; neither day nor night can reach it.

> Why fret away your life?
> See the willow tree by the river;
> There it is, watching the water flow by.

In this world, after all, what must be must be. Then why cannot we live with our mind so made up? "From where have you brought out such a question?"—this reply, as seemingly absurd as it may sound, is indeed the outburst of Ummon's heartfelt compassion, for he is trying to save us—by making us transcend time—from the grievous situation where we have lost our spiritual basis.

> The bell rings,
> Tonight again the bell rings—
> The toll in this ancient city!

Not as the sound counting time, but as the toll to awaken our inner life, I would like to listen to the resounding bell, alone in silence. If only for this little while, I want to be back to my original self, naked, face-to-face with the Absolute, entrusting the whole of my body and spirit to the eternal life.

Perhaps, thereupon, a whole new world may open up unto us.

SCRIPTURE OF NO LETTERS

Pure and fresh are the flowers with dew,
Clear and bright is the singing of the birds;
Clouds are calm, waters are blue.
Who has written the True Word of no letters?

Lofty are the mountains, green are the trees,
Deep are the valleys, lucid are the streams;
The wind is soft, the moon is serene.
Calmly I read the True Word of no letters.

Zenkei Shibayama

Other TUT BOOKS available:

Please order from your bookstore or write directly to:

CHARLES E. TUTTLE CO., INC.
Suido 1-chome, 2–6, Bunkyo-ku, Tokyo 112

or:

CHARLES E. TUTTLE CO., INC.
Rutland, Vermont 05701 U.S.A.